WEAPON

THE LEWIS GUN

NEIL GRANT

Series Editor Martin Pegler

First published in Great Britain in 2014 by Osprey Publishing,
PO Box 883, Oxford, OX1 9PL, UK
PO Box 3985, New York, NY 10185-3985, USA
E-mail: info@ospreypublishing.com

Osprey Publishing is part of the Osprey Group

A CIP catalogue record for this book is available from the British
Library

Print ISBN: 978 1 78200 791 3
PDF ebook ISBN: 978 1 78200 792 0
ePub ebook ISBN: 978 1 78200 793 7

Index by Alan Rutter
Typeset in Sabon and Univers
Battlescenes by Peter Dennis
Cutaway by Alan Gilliland
Originated by PDQ Media, Bungay, UK
Printed in China through Worldprint Ltd

14 15 16 17 18   10 9 8 7 6 5 4 3 2 1

Osprey Publishing is supporting the Woodland Trust, the UK's
leading woodland conservation charity, by funding the dedication
of trees.

www.ospreypublishing.com

Author's dedication

Dedicated to my father, Sergeant George Grant of the Welsh
Guards. Thanks, Dad.

Acknowledgements

The author and editor would like to thank the staff and trustees
of the Small Arms School Corps museum for their invaluable
assistance in the preparation of this book.

Imperial War Museum Collections

Many of the photos in this book come from the Imperial War
Museum's huge collections which cover all aspects of conflict
involving Britain and the Commonwealth since the start of the
twentieth century. These rich resources are available online to
search, browse and buy at www.iwmcollections.org.uk. In
addition to Collections Online, you can visit the Visitor Rooms
where you can explore over 8 million photographs, thousands of
hours of moving images, the largest sound archive of its kind in
the world, thousands of diaries and letters written by people in
wartime, and a huge reference library. To make an appointment,
call (020) 7416 5320, or e-mail mail@iwm.org.uk
Imperial War Museum www.iwm.org.uk

Front cover images are courtesy of (top) the Royal Armouries
(author's photograph, © Royal Armouries PR.7098) and
(bottom) the Imperial War Museum (© IWM Q 10609).

Editor's note

For ease of comparison please refer to the following conversion
table:
1 mile = 1.6km
1yd = 0.9m
1ft = 0.3m
1in = 2.54cm/25.4mm
1lb = 0.45kg

Artist's note

Readers may care to note that the original paintings from which
the battlescenes in this book were prepared are available for
private sale. All reproduction copyright whatsoever is retained
by the Publishers. All enquiries should be addressed to:

Peter Dennis, 'Fieldhead', The Park, Mansfield, Nottinghamshire
NG18 2AT, UK, or email magie.h@ntlworld.com

The Publishers regret that they can enter into no correspondence
upon this matter.

CONTENTS

INTRODUCTION

World War I did not see the first use of machine guns. The early hand-cranked repeaters such as the Gatling and Nordenfelt first appeared in the 1860s and 1870s, while the Maxim – the first true machine gun, in that it was operated purely by the energy produced by firing one cartridge working the action to load the next – had appeared in 1884. The British Army had used the Maxim to great effect against the Sudanese Mahdists at the battle of Omdurman in 1898, while US forces had used them (albeit less effectively) in the Spanish–American War of the same year. More recently, the Russo-Japanese War of 1904–05 had given observers from the Great Powers the chance to see machine guns used under the conditions that might prevail in a European war, though they did not necessarily draw all the correct lessons from what they saw.

World War I was the first war to be dominated by the use of machine guns, however. Along with quick-firing artillery, they changed the whole nature of the battlefield, leading to the evolution of elaborate trench lines and creating a strategic stalemate that lasted until broken by technical solutions (tanks) or tactical solutions (creeping barrages, storm-troop tactics) in 1917–18. Most of the participants began World War I with very similar machine guns – water-cooled Maxim derivatives for Britain, Germany and Russia, while the Austrians used the broadly similar Schwarzlose. Even the French Hotchkiss – although quite different mechanically and not water cooled – was still reasonably close in weight and performance, and was used in the same way tactically. All were bulky tripod-mounted weapons, capable of maintaining a heavy, sustained fire as long as the ammunition and cooling water held out; in August 1916, a company of the British Machine Gun Corps fired nearly a million rounds through its ten Vickers guns in one day, without a single serious stoppage.

Such guns made the old-fashioned massed infantry attacks almost prohibitively costly, and their use became more sophisticated as the war continued, to the point that they could be used to fire indirectly to interdict areas behind the enemy front line, in the manner of artillery. However, they had one key flaw; they were extremely heavy. The British Vickers was among the lightest, but still weighed just under 40lb, plus another 48lb for its tripod and 9lb for the water to fill its cooling jacket. It was man-portable only in the sense that its six-man crew could disassemble it and carry the gun, tripod and ammunition separately; it could not fire on the move.

While these medium machine guns remained in service until the end of the war, it became clear that another type of machine gun was also needed – a lighter, more portable gun that could go forward with attacking troops, carried and used by a single man. Developing such a gun proved problematic, however. The Germans produced the MG 08/15, a lightened version of their MG 08 medium machine gun, but this was poorly balanced, awkward to use, and still much too heavy at more than 50lb loaded. The French Chauchat CSRG was light enough, but chronically unreliable.

The best of the new breed was probably the Lewis gun, invented by an American, Isaac Newton Lewis. He initially offered it to the US Army, but after they showed little interest, he moved to Europe, where his gun was quickly adopted by the Belgians and then, with the outbreak of war, by the British. The Lewis's air-cooled design meant it was light enough to be carried and used on the move by a single man. It held its ammunition in 47-round pan magazines, easier to use on the move than the non-disintegrating fabric ammunition belts of the time, which tangled round the gunner's legs as he moved. It was reasonably reliable, though rather complex and stoppage-prone by the standards of World War II machine guns.

A British Lewis gun team on the Western Front, January 1918. For the first time, the Lewis would give infantry a machine gun light enough to go forward in the attack with them. (© IWM Q 10609)

New weapons required new tactics, and it took the British some time to learn how to get the best out of the Lewis's unique qualities, rather than simply regarding it as an inferior version of the trusty Vickers gun. Once they did work out the new tactics, the British issued Lewis guns on an ever-increasing scale, so that every infantry platoon had a Lewis gun by 1916, and two by the end of the war in 1918. The Lewis's compact and self-contained design led to it being mounted in a variety of tanks and armoured cars, and made it a natural choice for arming the new fighting aircraft. In the ultimate compliment, the Germans used every captured Lewis gun they could get their hands on, setting up a factory in Belgium to refurbish captured examples and convert them to fire German Mauser ammunition. Firing and maintaining the Lewis was even made part of their machine-gunners' training course.

The US Navy and Marines adopted the Lewis before American entry into World War I, but it saw little use except as an aerial gun; US Marines arriving in France in 1917 were outraged to find that their Lewis guns were withdrawn and replaced by inferior French Chauchat guns before they were sent into combat.

After World War I, the Lewis saw more hard use with British troops in the Middle East and on the North West Frontier, and with the US Marines in the 'Banana Wars' in Central America. It was also adopted by the Dutch, and by the Japanese, who issued it to their Special Naval Landing Forces and used it as an aerial gun. Despite replacing the Lewis with the Bren in front-line service, during World War II the British issued large numbers of Lewis guns to second-line troops and the Home Guard. The US Marines also used the Lewis in the early years of World War II, in the fierce fighting in the Philippines in 1941–42. In addition to this wide usage, it is difficult to think of a weapon with a better claim to be the first 'true' light machine gun, or to overestimate the effect it had on the development of modern small-scale infantry tactics.

The water-cooled British Vickers gun set up on its tripod. Although an excellent sustained-fire weapon, it could not be fired on the move and was too heavy to go forward with advancing infantry. (Neil Grant)

DEVELOPMENT
The first light machine gun

ORIGINS

Hiram Maxim often said that he abandoned his previous work on electricity and started developing his machine gun after being told by a friend 'Hang your chemistry and electricity! If you want to make a pile of money, invent something that will enable these Europeans to cut each others' throats with greater facility' (quoted in Ellis 1975: 34). While the story is almost certainly a later invention by Maxim himself, it does serve as a reminder that the first machine guns were not developed by armies, but by independent inventors who wanted to make money from their creations.[1]

Like any businessman, Maxim took out patents to protect his invention as completely as possible. As well as the recoil operation of his gun, he also patented the idea of using a water jacket to cool the barrel, and of feeding ammunition via fabric belts. Exactly as Maxim intended, these combined to make it difficult to design a viable machine gun without infringing at least one of his patents. This did not prevent aspiring inventors from trying to find other solutions, such as the metal feed strips used by the Hotchkiss gun instead of fabric belts.

The McClean gun

One of those inventors was an American physician, Dr Samuel McClean, who designed a machine gun, a 1-pdr (37mm) and a 3-pdr (47mm) automatic cannon, the latter intended to be mounted on a light truck. Although Dr McClean was able to secure substantial financial backing

---

1   Maxim was a prolific inventor; in addition to the machine gun, he was involved in pioneering work in mechanics and electricity, and invented things as diverse as the fire sprinkler, a coffee substitute and a successful amusement-park ride. He is often also credited with the invention of the silencer for firearms, but this was actually invented by his son, Hiram Percy Maxim.

over a number of years, allowing him to bring all his inventions to the prototype stage, none were adopted by any army.

The McClean machine gun was a gas-operated weapon, water cooled and fed from a 148-round helical drum above the barrel. However, it was an overly complicated design, and the prototypes performed poorly during a number of tests by the US Army and Navy, suffering repeated failures before firing more than 200–300 rounds. Even if the McClean gun had been tested successfully, it might still have fallen foul of Maxim's patents – Colt declined to purchase the McClean patents in 1909, William Skinner, President of Colt's, writing 'An examination of your patents convinces us that some of them are so near infringement of others it would be dangerous for us to attempt to acquire them' (quoted in Easterly 1998: 39). Dr McClean eventually lost control of both his patents and the company created to exploit them, and in December 1909 the company was dissolved, its remaining assets sold to cover its debts.

Lewis enters the scene

As a last-ditch effort to recover some of the money they had sunk into the McClean venture, the directors entered into discussion with Major Isaac Newton Lewis, a US Army officer who had been involved with the development and testing of the gun. Lewis observed correctly that the McClean in its current water-cooled form was inferior to the water-cooled guns already in service, but believed that it might have some hope as an air-cooled gun, and so, over the next weeks, Lewis developed an air-cooling system for the McClean gun. However, even with this new cooling system in place, the gun remained unreliable, and Lewis had to redesign the gas system and change the location of the mainspring. On the McClean gun,

The McClean gun in its original water-cooled form. Additional condenser coils beneath the water jacket were added for the later tests, without materially improving reliability. (Tom Laemlein/Armor Plate Press)

this had been a coil spring surrounding the gas piston, where it quickly heated up and lost temper as the weapon was fired. Lewis substituted a clock-type mainspring, located well away from the hot barrel in a round protrusion just ahead of the trigger. Finally, the unwieldy helical drum feed was replaced by a simpler spiral pan, holding 50 cartridges.

Lewis signed contracts in September 1910 with a new venture, the Automatic Arms Company, set up to exploit the McClean patents. Four prototype weapons were ordered from the well-known US-based Savage Arms Company, all chambered for the US .30-06 cartridge. Lewis had now been promoted to lieutenant colonel, but arranged for a year's leave of absence to develop and market the new gun, the prototypes of which were completed by early 1912.

Frustrations in the United States

Lewis used his influence with Major General Leonard Wood, the US Army's chief of staff, to arrange trials with the School of Musketry and the Artillery Board, rather than the Board of Ordnance. Lewis chose this unorthodox route as he believed that the Ordnance Department, which generally controlled Army weapons procurement, would not give his gun a fair trial, both because of past animosity with the departmental head, Brigadier General William Crozier, and because Lewis believed that the Ordnance Department was biased in favour of its major supplier, Colt's, which already produced the Benet-Mercie machine gun (see pages 22–23) for the Army.

Unsurprisingly, the Ordnance Department objected to the 'irregular' tests, and insisted that only the results of approved tests could be taken into consideration. Lewis and his backers attempted to arrange for a Lewis gun to be fired from an army aircraft but General Crozier blocked this, refusing to provide ammunition for the test, and proposing the use of the Benet-Mercie for aircraft trials instead. Without official permission, Lewis managed to arrange for his gun to be fired from an Army aircraft at the US Army's Pilot Training School in Maryland, apparently by convincing the school commander that a successful demonstration would make the US Army realize the potential military value of aircraft. The demonstration was a success, and attracted a great deal of publicity, which Lewis capitalized upon by claiming that in the future, armed aircraft would be able to inflict severe damage on capital ships. The US General Staff were unconvinced, however, and reiterated that they saw no combat role for aircraft. The Ordnance Department objections prevented any real progress by the time Lewis's leave of absence ran out in September 1912. Lewis returned briefly to duty, but, frustrated with the Army, he retired from active duty shortly afterwards and moved to Europe to market his gun there.

Progress in Europe

Meanwhile, the company had arranged trials with the British and Belgian armies, including firing from aircraft, using two of the Savage-produced .30-06 prototypes. While this did not lead to immediate orders, it did make both armies aware of the new weapon, and comments were

favourable enough that a European subsidiary (Armes Automatiques Lewis SA) was set up in Belgium. Initially, it was planned to set up a factory in the Belgian town of Liège, with its strong gun-making tradition, but Lewis struck a better deal with Birmingham Small Arms (BSA), the largest arms factory in Britain.

By mid-1913, BSA had delivered the first 50 guns, effectively handmade in seven different calibres. Armes Automatiques Lewis's sales machine now went into high gear. The company organized a large and successful demonstration at Bisley, the spiritual home of British rifle shooting, attended by British and foreign observers and press. Although no production guns were available, several armies expressed interest, including the British, who had no requirement for a light machine gun (LMG) for the infantry, but did see the potential of the lightweight Lewis as an aircraft weapon. Ironically, in the light of future events, the company also investigated the possibility of sales to Germany; their chief salesman was still there when the war broke out and only avoided internment by catching the last train leaving for Russia before the border closed.

INTO SERVICE

When Britain declared war on Germany on 4 August 1914, the Lewis gun was involved from the first. Five of the original prototypes (chambered for the 7.65×53mm Belgian cartridge) were supplied to the Belgian government the day after war broke out, followed by another 15 prototype guns in .303 British, and by 15 August they were being used by the Belgian forces defending Namur. The British War Office promptly bought every Lewis gun available, and had ordered more than 1,000 additional guns by the end of the year, followed by another 3,000 in 1915.

The British Lewis gun Mk I, produced by BSA of Birmingham. This particular gun features the oil bottle in the butt introduced in 1916, and has been retrofitted with the post-war stirrup grip, introduced in 1920. (Author's photograph, © Royal Armouries PR.7098)

The Model 1914/Mk I Lewis

The Model 1913 BSA guns were modified somewhat before entering mass production for British service – the diameter of the cooling fins and shroud was slightly reduced, the magazine was improved but reduced from 50-round capacity to 47, and the rear sight was changed. Most importantly, the action was redesigned so that the gun fired from an open bolt, leaving the empty chamber open to cool between firings. The modified guns (essentially, everything made after the first 50 prototypes) were marked by BSA as the Model 1914, and designated as the 'Gun, Lewis, .303-inch' by the Army; it was only referred to as the Mk I after the appearance of the Mk II in 1915.

At the start of the war, the British were desperate for as many Lewis guns as they could obtain. The main concern for BSA was keeping up with demand, particularly as they were also producing rifles for the expanding Army. As a result, BSA constructed a new purpose-built plant for the guns at its own expense, capable of turning out 150 Lewis guns per week. This was still not enough, and in 1915, government funding was agreed for a second, larger, plant, which would bring production up to 500 guns per week. By March 1916,

A BSA Mk I Lewis (with the butt replaced with a spade grip) showing the adapter used to mount the Lewis on the standard Mk IV Vickers tripod, and with an experimental 400-round magazine fitted. The latter was intended for use in fixed positions aboard aircraft; its height blocks the view through normal sights. (Author's photograph, © Royal Armouries PR.200 (gun), PR.201 (tripod) and PR.10159 (magazine))

BSA were producing 800 guns each week, and 1,000 per week by the end of the year. However, part of this demand was because orders for the heavier, water-cooled Vickers gun could not be fulfilled fast enough, and many of the first Lewis guns were issued with the heavy tripod designed for the Vickers. Without a tactical doctrine for LMGs, the guns were often initially used as Vickers substitutes, leading to complaints that the lighter Lewis was incapable of sustained fire, and too flimsy for field use. It was not until its unique advantages over the heavy Vickers – mobility and low profile – were appreciated that comments about the Lewis became more generally positive.

Another US disappointment

Popular mythology attributes US reluctance to adopt the Lewis to personal animosity on the part of Brigadier General Crozier, head of the US Ordnance Department. The two men certainly did dislike each other intensely, but the reality was not quite so simple. The US Army's experience with the air-cooled Benet-Mercie made decision-makers wary of adopting another air-cooled gun, and when the Lewis was finally tested in September 1913, as one of several possible replacements for the Benet-Mercie, the results were not positive. Against Lewis's express wishes, the Automatic Arms Company agreed to supply two BSA-made guns chambered for the US .30-06 cartridge. Lewis's concerns that the conversion to the more powerful US cartridge had not been sufficiently tested proved correct when the Lewis was eliminated after suffering 206 stoppages and 50 part breakages during the 20,000-round endurance test. It actually performed significantly worse than the Benet-Mercie being used as a control, which suffered 59 stoppages and seven breakages. The competition was eventually won by a version of the Vickers gun, to be produced under licence by Colt as the M1915.

THE LEWIS EXPOSED

.303in Lewis Mk I

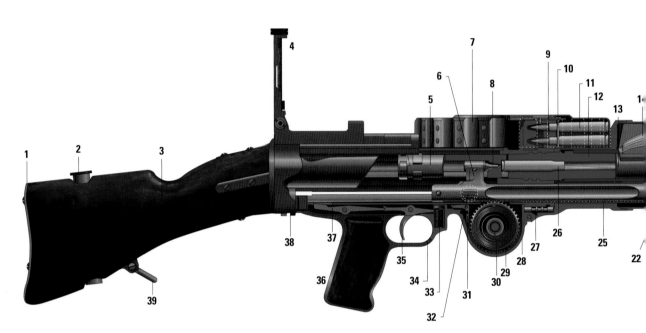

1.	Butt plate	**14.**	Radiator flanges	**27.**	Receiver locking pin
2.	Oil bottle	**15.**	Radiator casing	**28.**	Main spring casing
3.	Butt stock	**16.**	Gas vent	**29.**	Teeth on pinion
4.	Rear sight	**17.**	Bullet	**30.**	Main spring
5.	Bolt assembly	**18.**	Front sight	**31.**	Gear stop
6.	Striker post	**19.**	Barrel mouthpiece	**32.**	Slot for cocking handle
7.	Magazine assembly	**20.**	Front sling swivel	**33.**	Trigger spring
8.	Firing pin	**21.**	Gas chamber	**34.**	Trigger guard
9.	Magazine spacer ring assembly	**22.**	Piston rod	**35.**	Trigger
10.	Magazine separator pin	**23.**	Gas regulator key	**36.**	Pistol grip
11.	Cartridges in magazine	**24.**	Bipod	**37.**	Sear
12.	Bolt assembly	**25.**	Teeth on rack	**38.**	Butt latch
13.	Barrel	**26.**	Cartridge in chamber	**39.**	Rear sling swivel

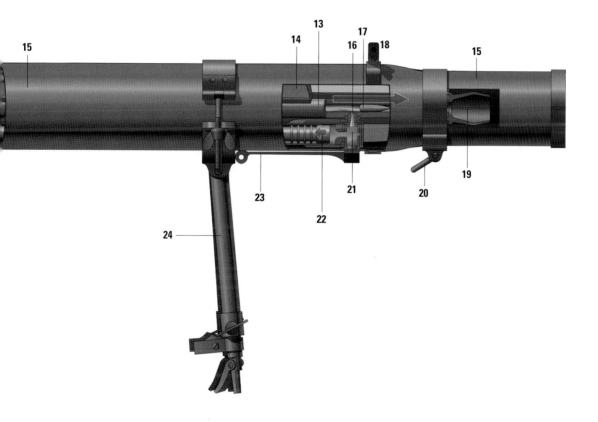

13 **14** **16** **17** **18** **15** **15**

23 **21** **20** **19**

22

24

The largest manufacturer of the Lewis gun was BSA in England, which produced roughly 145,000 guns. Production for the British government ended in 1919, but BSA continued to look for further orders until the eve of World War II. The American Savage Arms Company manufactured guns in .303 calibre for the British and Canadian forces, as well as just under 50,000 in .30-06 calibre for the US forces. The Savage plant ended Lewis gun production for the USA in June 1918, the production line being turned over to make BARs.

The French-based Hotchkiss firm negotiated to start manufacturing the Lewis in France, but the French government were adamant that Hotchkiss should concentrate on manufacturing as many of their standard M1914 tripod-mount guns as possible, so only around 4,400 aerial-type Lewis guns were produced in France, mostly by the little-known Darne Company.

Dutch Lewis guns were produced after World War I by the Dutch State Arsenal, Artillerie Inrichtingen. Production levels were quite low (fewer than 10,000 guns), but the arsenal was still producing guns when the Netherlands fell in 1940, and made its last orders for the Germans.

Portuguese troops armed with Savage-made Lewis guns in June 1917. The Portuguese supplied a small contingent to fight on the Western Front, and were mostly equipped by the British and French. (Tom Laemlein/Armor Plate Press)

The Canadian Savage-Lewis

With the outbreak of war, Canada began to raise troops to fight alongside those of the mother country, but machine guns to equip them were scarce. The Canadian government initially bought old-fashioned Colt machine guns from the neutral United States as a stopgap, while more modern guns were sourced. The American Savage Arms Company agreed to produce Lewis guns to the BSA pattern and chambered for the standard British .303 round. The Canadians ordered the first 500 guns from Savage in July 1915, and the gun was designated the Model 1915. Savage promised it would be so close to the BSA Model 1914 guns that parts would be interchangeable between the two. In practice, however, this remained an aspiration rather than a reality.

Since Savage Arms could produce more guns than the Canadians needed, the War Office in Britain – who still wanted more guns than BSA could manufacture, even at their expanded plant – contracted Savage to produce guns for Britain, too. Savage also agreed to supply the French government with a small number of Lewis guns (in .303 British) for aerial use, since the standard French machine guns were ill-suited to that role: the Hotchkiss was too heavy and fed from strips, while the Chauchat was awkward, unreliable and its magazine size was limited by the sharp taper of the old-fashioned 8mm Lebel cartridge. Some 2,000 infantry-model guns were also supplied to Italy, where they were stripped for aircraft use. There were quality-control issues around poor heat-treating and parts fit with some Savage-produced guns, which hindered US adoption of the weapon and led to some of the Savage guns having to be rebuilt at BSA.

Aerial Lewis guns – the Mk II, Mk II* and Mk III

The Lewis became the first machine gun to be used from an aircraft, when Lewis arranged for it to be taken aloft in a Wright Pusher B aircraft at the US Army's Pilot Training School in July 1912. It was an unmodified ground gun, and used purely to attack a ground target – a 6ft by 7ft sheet of cloth laid out in a field – but clearly demonstrated how aircraft could be used in a future war. As Lewis said in a press interview following the flight, 'Aircraft can no longer be unarmed in wartime and used only for scouting purposes' (quoted in Easterly 1998: 63). His words were to come true within a very few years – as opposing scout aircraft met each other over the trenches in the first days of the war, pilots and observers armed themselves with pistols and rifles, then began to look for more powerful weapons.

With its light weight and self-contained design – no fabric belts to tangle or flap in the slipstream, no cooling water to spill or require condensers – the Lewis was the obvious choice for an aircraft gun. As a result, it was quickly adopted even by countries that did not use it as an infantry gun, such as France, Italy and Russia. These generally kept the chambering for the British .303 round, though some of the guns made for the Russians were redesigned to take their 7.62×54mm rimmed cartridges.

The first airborne Lewis guns were simply ground models, sometimes with a spade grip at the rear instead of the butt and perhaps a simple cloth bag added to catch spent cases that might damage the engine or propeller. Experiments by pilots – sometimes unsanctioned by higher authority – prompted attempts to adapt the guns to their new role, often by cutting the barrel shroud and radiator fins back drastically. This saved a significant amount of weight (typically 3–4lb), and also reduced the slipstream drag on the barrel, allowing the observer to track a moving aircraft more easily.

These changes were soon formalized into the Lewis Mk II, a purpose-built aerial gun issued from mid-1915. This eliminated the radiator fins completely, but kept a narrow shroud around the barrel to protect the gas tube. It could be fitted with an improved wire-stiffened bag to catch spent cases, and special air sights. A larger 97-round drum was also produced for the air gun from early 1916; the magazine peg had to be extended to accept the larger magazine, which was not usable with the standard infantry gun. A later Mk II* version, issued from 1918, was modified for a higher rate of fire.

In May 1918, the Mk III aerial gun appeared, superseding the Mk II in production, though guns already issued

A gunner demonstrates the stance necessary to use the rear-firing Lewis gun aboard a Royal Flying Corps FE2d 'pusher' aircraft. Precarious enough in this posed shot on the ground, it must have been terrifying while aboard an aircraft in flight and probably manoeuvring to avoid being hit. Oddly, this particular aircraft has a Mk III Lewis on the rear mount, but a Mk II (with case-catcher bag) on the front.
(© IWM Q 69650)

TOP

A typical example of a Mk I ground-model Lewis gun 'stripped' for aerial use by removing the barrel casing and radiator fins. The rear portion of each of the radiator fins has been left intact, as they supported the gun's mounting ring. This particular example was made in Britain, but supplied to (and modified by) the Italian Air Service, as can be seen from the unique Italian wind vane sights. (Author's photograph, © Royal Armouries PR.7125)

MIDDLE

The Mk II was the first factory-produced aerial version of the Lewis. The radiator fins were removed, and although it retained a thin steel jacket of reduced diameter, this merely served to protect the barrel. This particular gun is fitted with a wire-stiffened case-catcher bag, and the enlarged trigger guard to allow use while wearing flying gloves. The magazine here is the early (non-fluted) version of the 47-round drum; most aircraft guns used the larger 97-round drum. (Author's photograph, © Royal Armouries PR.7126)

BOTTOM

The Mk III was the final aerial version of the Lewis, and did away entirely with the barrel jacket to reduce drag, though some units fitted wooden barrel protectors to prevent damage to the vulnerable gas tube. The magazine fitted is the 97-round Mk II Aero drum. (Author's photograph, © Royal Armouries PR.8015)

remained in use. The main improvement over the Mk II was again an increased rate of fire, to score more hits in the short period the gunner had an enemy aircraft in his sights. Visually, the main difference was that the barrel shroud was now completely removed, leaving the barrel and gas tube exposed, though some were fitted with wooden forestocks.

Another US trial

Despite selecting the M1915 Vickers after the 1913–14 trials, the US Army wanted to re-test the Lewis in 1915–16, apparently because of the positive reports of its performance during the fighting in Europe. Ironically, when the Ordnance Department requested that Savage supply weapons for further testing, Savage responded that they were too occupied with their current production commitments to spare even one gun. In January 1916, General Crozier testified before the Senate Committee on Military Affairs, which criticized his department's failure to plan for equipping the expanded US Army needed for any foreign commitment, particularly the lack of suitable machine guns. Pancho Villa's attack on Columbus two months later and the ensuing 'Daylight Gun' controversy did nothing to defuse the situation.

Savage finally supplied two Lewis guns for testing in April 1916, one chambered for British .303 ammunition, the other for the US .30-06 round. The .303 Lewis performed reliably, but the .30-06 model performed very poorly once more, with numerous stoppages and parts breakages. The test board noted the lightness and simplicity of the Lewis, but felt that it needed more development by Savage for the US cartridge before it would be acceptable as a service weapon. However, three guns in British .303 calibre were purchased for trials with units along the Mexican border. Meanwhile, General Wood, still sympathetic to Lewis, organized a comparative test at Plattsburgh, New York, between the Benet-Mercie and a pair of .303 Lewis guns, which found the Lewis to be superior. General Crozier denounced the test as unauthorized and improper, sparking ill-tempered exchanges in the press that reached the front pages of *The New York Times* until both officers were formally ordered to desist by Secretary of War Newton D. Baker.

With production of the M1915 Colt version of the Vickers yet to start, and a shortage of any machine guns at all to equip the troops setting out on the punitive expedition into Mexico under General Pershing, Savage agreed with the British government to divert up to 1,500 .303-calibre

US cavalrymen during the 1916 US expedition into Mexico to hunt down Pancho Villa after the attack on Columbus, Texas. They took with them 350 Savage-made Lewis guns, chambered for the .303in British cartridge. (Tom Laemlein/Armor Plate Press)

Lewis guns from the British order to the United States, though ultimately General Crozier ordered only 350 guns. Combat experience with the Lewis in Mexico was mixed, with some units finding it unreliable due to poor quality control, a problem that also affected guns produced by Savage for the British and Canadians.

The US Navy had conducted its own tests, and found the .303 Savage Lewis good enough to order some .30-06 guns for further testing. In April 1917, after the United States entered the war and found itself still desperately short of any machine guns, since none of the Colt-made M1915 Vickers had been delivered, the Ordnance Department ordered another 1,300 .30-06 Savage Lewis guns, on the basis of the successful testing by the Navy.

By this time, the gas system of the .30-06 Savage guns had been properly modified to cope with the more powerful US cartridge, which resolved the reliability problems, and a final test by the Ordnance Board in May 1917 accepted the modified guns as highly satisfactory.

Into US service – the M1917 and M1918

However, the Lewis guns ordered would not be available in quantity until 1918, while the newly developed water-cooled M1917 Browning machine gun and M1918 Browning Automatic Rifle (BAR) would only arrive towards the end of that year. The United States was forced, therefore, to adopt the French Chauchat CSRG as a stopgap, and assigned most of the Lewis guns produced to be aircraft guns, since the Chauchat could not sensibly be used in this role. While this decision was criticized by Lewis's allies after the war, the faults of the Chauchat were not generally known at the time, and later arguments that the Lewis should have been adopted for both aerial and infantry use ignore the realities of the limited number of guns available at that point.

The US M1917 (known as the 'Mk VI' to the US Navy) closely resembled the British Mk I infantry gun, though there were differences in detail (the M1917 gas regulator had four holes rather than two as on the original British version, had slightly fewer aluminium radiator fins inside the barrel jacket and could only be cocked from the left side, for instance) and parts were not interchangeable between the two. Since the M1917 was used largely as an aircraft gun, many were stripped down to remove the radiator vanes in the same way as British guns. A purpose-built air gun (the M1918) was introduced the following year.

US Lewis guns (in this case a US Navy Mk VI) differed most visibly from British ones in having a metal reinforce around the waist of the stock, and omitted the right-hand cocking slot. This example is fitted with an adjustable-leg bipod similar to the British pattern. (Author's photograph, © Royal Armouries PR.7037)

The Lewis gun described

There were several notable features in the Lewis design. The most obvious is that it was air cooled. This made it significantly lighter than water-cooled guns such as the Vickers, but air is much less efficient at drawing heat away from a hot barrel than water. Lewis therefore developed a system of forced air cooling. The barrel of the Lewis gun was surrounded by fins, to maximize the surface area for heat to radiate away from. These fins were made of aluminium, which has six times the heat conductivity of steel, and were enclosed in a tubular shroud extending several inches past the end of the barrel. When the gun fired, the muzzle blast created a temporary vacuum inside the end of the cooling shroud, pulling cool air from the breech end along the cooling fins.

As well as being several times more efficient than simple air cooling, the extension of the shroud past the end of the barrel meant that it also operated as an effective flash hider, making the muzzle flash difficult to see except from directly in front, and reduced the muzzle blast and noise for the gunner. Some claimed that the cooling shroud was ineffective, pointing out that it was often removed from aerial guns, and these weapons continued to function perfectly well when converted back to ground use. However, the point of the shroud is not that the gun needed it to function, but that it prolonged the time the gun could continue to fire before overheating.

The Lewis gun was fed from a top-mounted pan magazine, holding 47 rounds in two layers, though most aerial guns used a 97-round drum holding four layers of cartridges. Unlike most magazines, the Lewis drum contains no springs to feed the cartridges. Instead, a feed arm on the top of the receiver is actuated mechanically by the gun mechanism to feed cartridges into the action. The outside of the pan actually rotates while firing – the reverse of a normal magazine, where the outer casing remains still and the rounds are moved by internal springs. The pan magazine had several advantages over the fabric belts used in the Vickers gun, which often absorbed moisture in the damp conditions of the trenches and swelled up or froze solid, and it eliminated the problem of lengths of expended belt hanging from the gun that dogged the German MG 08/15. It also meant that the gun would theoretically feed at any angle, even upside down, whereas a belt feed would jam, making the Lewis especially suitable for aerial use. However, it was not without disadvantages. The open-bottomed design of the pan made it easy for mud to get onto the cartridges and clog the gun, causing stoppages, and the sheet-metal drums themselves were easily deformed by impacts, which would make them useless.

The Lewis is a gas-operated weapon – the normal choice for machine guns today, but a significant change from most machine guns of its time, which were recoil-operated Maxim derivatives. A gas block near the muzzle (normally hidden by the cooling sleeve) taps off some of the expanding gas from each fired cartridge, and uses it to push back a gas piston, chambering the next round and re-cocking the gun for the next shot.

The Lewis featured an unusual design of return spring. Most designs utilize a straight spring housed in the butt, but the Lewis has a spiral, clock-type spring, located in the semicircular hump on the bottom of the receiver, just ahead of the trigger. The spring sat inside and operated a gear wheel, which meshed with a toothed rack machined on the underside of the gas-piston rod. The return spring was wound when the gas piston was pushed back by the tapped-off propellant gases and then unwound itself with the closing movement of the rotating bolt group, which was locked into recesses in the receiver walls by four radial lugs.

As well as being complex, this arrangement put the spring close to the breech, where it heated up and gradually lost its temper as the gun fired, eventually causing a stoppage. On the other hand, the design meant that the wooden butt could easily be removed and replaced with a spade grip, which could not be done with a Bren gun.

The underside of a Lewis gun, showing the aluminium cooling fins surrounding the barrel inside the cooling shroud and the 'hump' containing the clock-type mainspring just ahead of the trigger guard. (Neil Grant)

THE LEWIS'S RIVALS AND COMPARATORS

The Benet-Mercie

The US Army had been the earliest adopter of rapid-fire guns, in the form of the manually cranked multi-barrel Gatling, a weapon that it had used during the Spanish–American War and subsequent Philippine–American War of 1898–1902. In 1904 the Gatling was replaced by an extremely heavy version of the Maxim (62lb for the gun alone, or 142lb on its tripod), but the cavalry (still influential as a legacy of the US Army's recent past as an Indian-fighting constabulary) argued that this was impracticably heavy for their use, and campaigned for a lighter machine gun. Rather than developing a specialist LMG for cavalry use, the assumption that a single machine gun should be able to fulfil all roles led the USA to adopt a lightweight version of the Hotchkiss machine gun as a replacement for all machine guns then in service.

The weapon was known in the United States as the M1909 Benet-Mercie Machine Rifle after its designers; Lawrence Benet was the son of a previous head of the US Ordnance Department, and a reminder of his involvement could not have hurt during the adoption process. It was a light (27lb) air-cooled and gas-operated weapon, feeding from 30-round brass strips of cartridges rather than a belt. Complaints soon emerged about the fragility, poor accuracy and limited sustained-fire performance of the gun, though the latter was an inevitable consequence of its light, air-cooled design. The issues with the Benet-Mercie came to a head in March 1916, when a force of Mexican revolutionaries led by Pancho Villa

US Marines with a Benet-Mercie LMG at Parris Island in 1918; although superseded in front-line use by this date, it was still used for training. Note the rigid metal 30-round feed strip emerging from the side of the gun, and the second strip held by the loader. (Tom Laemlein/Armor Plate Press)

launched a night attack on the border town of Columbus, New Mexico and the nearby Army post. While the raiders were driven off with heavy losses, the performance of the Benet-Mercie machine guns used by the Army was heavily criticized. In particular, the inexperienced crews accidentally loaded the weapon's metal feed strips into the guns upside down, then struggled to clear the resulting jams in the dark, leading to the weapon being lampooned in the press as the 'Daylight Gun' because of its apparent uselessness at night.

The problems encountered with the Benet-Mercie seem to have been due not so much to an intrinsic problem with the gun as to poor training and miserly allowances of practice ammunition, exacerbated by the common US Army practice of assigning misfits and other unwanted men to the machine-gun platoon to prevent them interfering with the proper running of the rifle companies. The British cavalry purchased a .303 version of the same weapon as the Hotchkiss Mk I in 1916, and with better-trained crews, they do not seem to have experienced any significant problems. More than 30,000 of these were produced, many of them to be used as tank machine guns in the same way as the Lewis. Late in the war, the rigid metal feed strips were supplemented by a 50-round flexible belt created by articulating multiple three-round strips together.

The Chauchat CSRG

The French Chauchat CSRG Mle 1915 was the most-produced LMG of World War I, with almost 260,000 manufactured. It served with both the French and American armies, despite being commonly regarded as among the worst LMGs ever designed. The Chauchat's barrel was a shortened Lebel rifle barrel, while the rest of the gun was made from simple steel stampings and tubing by a company which had previously made bicycles; one of the Chauchat's few virtues was its relatively light (9kg, or 21lb) weight. It was chambered for the standard French 8mm Lebel cartridge. This was an old-fashioned round, so sharply tapered that the 20-round magazines were actually semicircular, curving round to meet the receiver at both ends. Unfortunately, this prevented the front handgrip being installed anywhere near the point of balance, making the gun awkward to hold, let alone shoot accurately.

It was designed around an unusually long recoil action, which meant that the recoil spring partly overhung the butt. In consequence, any firer holding it in a conventional position to use the (rather poor) sights risked a bruising blow to his cheek every time he fired – an occurrence common enough to acquire its own nickname, 'la gifle' to French gunners, the 'Sho-Sho Smack' to Americans. The sides of the magazines were pierced by large cut-outs, apparently to save weight and so that the user could see how much ammunition was left. In practice, they simply allowed dirt to get into the action and jam the gun.

The Lewis compared

Weapon	Calibre	Feed	Rate of fire	Cooling	Weight (unloaded)	Remarks
Vickers Mk I (British, 1912)	.303 (7.7×56mm)	250-rd fabric belt	450rds/min	Water	39lb 13oz	Fired from a tripod; 99lb 7oz with tripod and full water jacket
Lewis Mk I (British, 1914)	.303 (7.7×56mm)	47-rd pan	550rds/min	Forced-air	25lb 15oz	The US M1917 is very similar, but in .30-06 calibre
Lewis Mk II (British, 1916)	.303 (7.7×56mm)	97-rd aerial pan	550rds/min	Air	18lb 8oz	Versions of this were used by several other countries
MG 08/15 (German, 1916)	7.92×57mm Mauser	100-rd fabric belt	450rds/min	Water	17.8kg (39lb 3oz)	20.8kg (45lb 12oz) with full water jacket; could use the Mauser MG 08's 250-rd fabric belt, but firing on the move would have been impractical
Mle 1915 Chauchat CSRG (French, 1915)	8×50mm Lebel	20-rd box magazine	240rds/min	Air	9.5kg (20lb 14oz)	Also used by the US forces, in both 8mm Lebel and .30-06
Benet-Mercie (US, 1909)	.30-06 (7.62×63mm)	30-rd metal strip	600rds/min	Air	26lb 13oz	An almost identical weapon was used by British cavalry as the Hotchkiss Portative, in .303
M1918 BAR (US, 1918)	.30-06 (7.62×63mm)	20-rd box magazine	550rds/min	Air	15lb 7oz	Provided suppressive fire from the hip and so lacked a bipod, though later versions did feature one, along with an adjustable rate of fire
Bren Mk I (British, 1937)	.303 (7.7×56mm)	30-rd box magazine	500rds/min	Air	22lb 3oz	Air cooling supplemented by quick-change barrel

The 8mm Lebel version of the Chauchat CSRG automatic rifle. Note the awkwardly placed front grip just ahead of the pistol grip, and the large slots in the side of the sharply curved magazines, which let dirt into the mechanism. (Neil Grant)

In fairness, the Chauchat was actually designed as an automatic rifle, rather than a true LMG. It was intended to provide 'walking fire' in the same way as the later US BAR, rather than sustained fire. It was adopted by the Americans by default, since the United States entered the war lacking sufficient machine guns or artillery and purchased both from the French. Most US troops received the regular 8mm Lebel version, but some received the M1918 version chambered for the US .30-06 cartridge. The redesign was poorly done; the American inspectors at the

manufacturing plant rejected up to 40 per cent of the weapons coming off the line as unfit for service, and the 60 per cent they passed proved even less reliable than the lacklustre French original. Around 18,000 of the Mle 1918 version were produced before it was replaced in US service by the BAR, and many of the most vociferous criticisms (and stories of jammed guns simply being thrown away) actually relate to this version.

Neither version of the Chauchat had a long service-life; while most of the World War I-era LMGs soldiered on into the 1930s, the French and Americans replaced the Chauchat almost immediately after the war was over. Ironically, as most were scrapped rather than put into storage, the Chauchat is now among the rarest and least-encountered of the World War I machine guns.

The MG 08/15

The Germans also identified the need for an LMG, but came to a very different solution. As well as purchasing Madsen LMGs from Denmark and pressing captured Lewis guns into service, they also created a lightened version of their standard machine gun, the Maxim-derived MG 08. The heavy sled mount was removed, the original trigger and spade grips were replaced by a shoulder stock and a new pistol grip and trigger were added underneath the weapon, allowing it to be fired from a bipod or even a shoulder sling.

Using the standard machine gun as a starting point simplified training and spare-part manufacture, but it also brought significant disadvantages. The original MG 08 was a notably heavy gun (over 58lb dry and unloaded even without its heavy sled mount, compared to just under 40lb for the British Vickers). While the designers reduced the capacity of the water jacket and slimmed and lightened the receiver, the resulting gun still weighed nearly 53lb with a full belt and water jacket, almost twice the weight of a loaded Lewis gun. Firing on the move was difficult since the MG 08/15 used a shortened 100-round version of the 250-round non-disintegrating fabric belt used by the MG 08. While a sheet-metal belt carrier was fixed to the right side of the gun to hold the fresh belt, the expended portion trailed from the left side of the gun after the cartridges had been fired, tangling in the gunner's legs.

Despite these shortcomings, large numbers of MG 08/15s were produced, with each infantry company receiving six by 1918, and their extremely solid construction meant that some soldiered on long after World War I. An air-cooled version without the water-cooling jacket – the MG 08/18 – was produced in small numbers at the end of the war, but while this was significantly lighter at 38lb loaded, the barrel overheated too quickly.

The German MG 08/15. Despite the butt, pistol grip and slimmed-down water-cooling jacket, its origins as a lightened version of the Maxim-derived MG 08 are obvious, making descriptions of it as a 'Light Machine Gun' somewhat optimistic. (Neil Grant)

'The BSA .5-inch machine gun' as illustrated in the 1921 BSA brochure. Although not a straight upscaling of the Lewis mechanism, the similarities of this design to the BSA-produced Lewis gun are readily apparent. (Neil Grant)

The BSA 'Twin Lewis' prototype, essentially two modified Mk III aerial guns mounted belly-to-belly and fired by a single trigger in an effort to increase the defensive firepower a single aircraft gunner could produce. (Author's photograph, © Royal Armouries PR.7106)

AFTER WORLD WAR I

Post-war developments

Lewis gun production in Britain and the United States ended shortly after the Armistice. However, there were several programmes to upgrade the large existing stock of Lewis guns held by the British forces. New accessories appeared, including a stirrup grip that attached to the barrel shroud to make firing on the move easier. The strangest, however, must have been a hand-cranked rattle that was attached to the side of the gun to simulate the sound of machine-gun fire during exercises. Most of the changes proposed to the gun itself never got past the experimental stage, such as a single-shot mechanism and a belt-fed version using an early version of the metal disintegrating-link ammunition belt.

BSA also produced a new 'Light Infantry Model' of the Lewis, with a simple wooden forestock replacing the barrel shroud and radiator fins, using the single-shot mechanism mentioned above to avoid overheating and an experimental 22-round semi-disposable pan magazine (effectively a single-row feed strip made in circular form) to deal with the perennial issue of damage to the standard drums. It was produced in response to criticism over the Lewis's weight (reduced to 17lb in the Light Infantry Model), but since the Lewis was still complex and stoppage-prone, the British Army test board felt that adopting a .303 version of the American BAR would have been a better way to achieve the same weight reduction. Aerial guns received enlarged trigger guards to make operation easier while wearing thick flying gloves. A BSA prototype for a high-speed twin aircraft gun – with the barrels mounted base-to-base so that the ammunition drums were mounted vertically on each side like wagon wheels – was discarded after poor performance in trials, however.

In 1921, BSA produced a gun based on the Lewis, but chambered for the .50 Vickers round. According to the sales brochure, it was intended for use against aircraft and tanks. The gun fed from a Lewis-style 37-round drum magazine, and many features were strongly reminiscent

of the Lewis, but significant internal changes meant the gun was not simply the Lewis scaled up. The .50 Vickers round (12.7×81mm) was significantly less powerful than the round developed for the belt-fed .50 Browning (12.7×99mm), which was already in production, and the BSA gun found no takers.

Replacement by the Bren

With thousands of Lewis guns left over from World War I, and military spending under such pressure during the Great Depression that troops' pay was cut, the War Office made no real attempt to replace the Lewis during the 1920s. By 1930, however, the Lewis was looking increasingly dated, and the remaining stock of guns was starting to wear out. The War Office therefore issued a requirement for a new weapon to replace both the Lewis and the heavier Vickers gun. These trials ultimately led to the selection of the Bren gun, adopted in 1935. The Bren was simpler and more dependable than the Lewis, and its quick-change barrel – a good crew could swap a barrel red-hot from firing for a cool spare one in six to eight seconds – allowed a far greater sustained-fire capability than the Lewis could achieve, though it never fully replaced the Vickers.

Despite this, BSA put forward a new version of the Lewis in 1937. It was a radical redesign, replacing the troublesome clock-type mainspring and pan magazine with a straight spring in the butt and a curved box magazine, both features used on the Bren. The weight was also reduced drastically, to 21lb. There was still no quick-change barrel, but the sales brochure made a virtue out of necessity, commenting, 'The design does not allow the quick replacement of a hot barrel, as in the role of a light machine gun such quick replacement is not considered necessary ... in the stress of battle, even with a quick barrel change, the firer will normally carry on with one barrel, having no time to replace it with the spare' (quoted in Easterly 1998: 284). The design attracted little official or foreign interest, however.

The last of the aerial Lewis guns became obsolete a few years after the infantry version, replaced by new guns with a higher rate of fire such as the Vickers Gas Operated (also known as the Vickers 'K'), adopted in 1937. Another British firm, the Soley Armament Company, put forward proposals for converting surplus Mk III aircraft Lewis guns for infantry use.

The BSA 1940 pattern followed on from the 1937 pattern in replacing the distinctive Lewis drum feed and clock-type mainspring with a Bren-type box magazine and straight mainspring in the butt, although it still lacked the quick-change barrel of the Bren. The Army was not interested, preferring actual Bren guns to substitutes. (Author's photograph, © Royal Armouries PR. 7105)

The old and the new juxtaposed, as a Lewis gun team in pre-war service dress are supported by a Universal Carrier on an exercise in Hampshire in 1938. Two years later, the men would be a Bren team in battledress, the road signs would have disappeared to add to the confusion of any lost German paratroopers, and everyone would be referring to the vehicle as a 'Bren Carrier'. (© IWM H 275)

Their first prototype shortened the barrel and replaced the drum magazine with a Bren-type curved box, while the second prototype also replaced the clock-type mainspring with a more conventional type. Neither performed well, and even after a third prototype achieved better results, the War Office made it clear that it would rather concentrate on producing actual Bren guns rather than substitutes.

World War II Lewis guns

Although the Bren had been adopted as a replacement for the Lewis before the war, the first Brens were not delivered until September 1937, and the 30,000-odd produced by the start of the war were almost all taken to France with the British Expeditionary Force (BEF) and lost in the retreat to Dunkirk. With fewer than 2,300 Bren guns left to defend against anticipated German invasion, the British began a crash programme to simplify the Bren and speed up production, but in the interim, the Lewis helped plug the gap. It soldiered on with Regular Army units in the Middle East until 1941–42, when enough Bren guns finally became available, and as air defence for Royal Air Force (RAF) units and naval vessels until the end of the war.

The final version of the Soley-Lewis, a privately developed proposal to modernize existing Lewis guns for infantry use. The British government showed little interest in the proposal, preferring to concentrate on producing Bren guns, and very few were converted. (Author's photograph, © Royal Armouries PR.7104)

Home Guard learning to use a Mk III aircraft Lewis gun under the supervision of a Regular in 1940. The gun is fitted with a 97-round drum and a muzzle booster to increase rate of fire. The second crewman is using his left hand to stabilize the sometimes-wobbly 'music stand' anti-aircraft tripod; he should have a spare magazine in his right hand, ready for a quick change. (© IWM H 4062)

The Mk III* was a conversion of the US .30-06 Savage Model 1918 aerial gun into a substitute infantry LMG by grafting a skeleton butt to the rear of the spade grip, and attaching a bipod. Note the wooden block at the top of the skeleton butt, provided to allow the weapon to be fired using the infantry grip. The .303 Mk III** was very similar. (Author's photograph, © Royal Armouries PR. 7101)

The major users of the Lewis, however, were the Home Guard. As well as the thousands of obsolete Lewis guns left in Army stocks, the government also purchased 25,000 BARs and 46,000 Lewis guns from the United States. The US guns were all marked with a red band around the stock and a red dot on the centre of each magazine, to indicate that they were chambered for the American .30-06 round.

Converting aerial guns back to ground use

Many of the Lewis guns issued to the Home Guard were obsolete aerial guns, of both British and US patterns, with a spade rear grip rather than a butt and lacking both cooling fins and bipods. A few were fully converted back to infantry specifications using spare parts from remaining stocks, but most were quickly converted for ground use as the Mk III* (US .30-06 calibre) and Mk III** (British .303 calibre). The conversion was almost identical, the only difference between the two being the calibre of the base gun. A strap metal skeleton butt was added on to the rear of the spade grip, a simple wood block forend was added under the gas cylinder, and a basic bipod attached in front of it. Sights varied, some guns being fitted with basic fixed-aperture sights that prevented the use of the 97-round aerial drum, with other guns being fitted with simple anti-aircraft sights. A slightly different conversion (with wooden butt and forward pistol grip) was issued for close anti-aircraft defence to Merchant Navy ships as the Mk III DEMS (standing for 'Defensively Equipped Merchant Ships').

The last-ditch Lewis – the Mk IV

Not all of the Lewis guns in storage were complete or usable, and the stocks of components such as the clock-type mainspring were quickly exhausted. The Mk IV was a more radical conversion intended to bring such otherwise unusable guns into service. It used a skeleton butt and pistol grip made from strip steel, a simple triangular bipod and a straight mainspring mounted in a tube through the skeleton butt. Though ugly, the Mk IV represented a triumph of creating a usable weapon from insufficient parts and materials. It is probably as well that none actually needed to be used in combat, but they would have been much better than nothing, had the expected German invasion of Britain taken place.

OPPOSITE

A Yeoman of Signals on the bridge of the British destroyer HMS *Wolfhound* aims a Lewis gun DEMS (Defensively Equipped Merchant Ship) conversion, easily distinguishable from other conversions of aerial Lewis guns by its front pistol grip. (© IWM A 27255)

The Mk IV was a 'last ditch' weapon, produced from damaged or incomplete aerial guns by adding a simple butt, bipod and pistol grip manufactured from steel strip, and replacing the clock-type mainspring (often worn out or broken) with a straight Bren-type mainspring, contained in the tube running through the butt. (Author's photograph, © Royal Armouries PR.7099)

USE
Bringing firepower out of the trenches

FIRING THE LEWIS

The Lewis was generally fired from its bipod; with the ability to fire from the prone position, the Lewis gunner was much less exposed than the Vickers gunner, who fired from the sitting position. The bipod legs were independently adjustable, and terminated in spikes to grip the ground, with flip-down 'feet' intended to prevent the bipod sinking into soft mud. These were rarely as effective as the designers hoped, and gunners sometimes put wooden boards under the bipod feet to prevent them sinking into the muddy ground common on the Western Front.

To load the Lewis, the gunner (or his No. 2) placed the pan magazine on top of the magazine pillar, taking care to align the spline on the pillar with the slot in the central hole of the magazine. Once the magazine was in place, the gunner pulled back the cocking handle to draw the bolt to the rear, ready to load and fire the first round. The cocking handle was normally fitted on the left side of the weapon, but could be swapped over to the right, for example on guns fitted to twin mountings.

The sights on the infantry version of the Lewis were a fixed front post, and a ladder-type back sight, which was folded down for carriage or flicked up for use, and calibrated from 400yd to 2,100yd. The gunner could adjust it for range by moving the slider on the back sight up or down in 100yd increments until it corresponded to his estimate of the range to the target. (Sights need to be adjusted because gravity and air resistance mean that bullets actually travel in a parabola, rather than a straight line. Adjusting the sights changes the point of aim to compensate for this.)

The Lewis did not have a single-shot setting, though an experienced shot could squeeze off a single round by careful trigger control; betting on their ability to do this seems to have been a fairly standard way for Lewis gun instructors to win beer money off their trainees.

Belgian sailors learning to use Lewis guns in 1945 at a training establishment set up at the former Butlin's Holiday Camp at Skegness in Lincolnshire. Note the firing grip, and the raised ladder-type back sight, adjustable for range by moving a slider up and down. The circular depression on the stock was a modification introduced after World War I, and intended to take a brass disc identifying weapon and unit. (© IWM D 24885)

The safety catch was a simple bar above the trigger; it was pushed upwards to physically lock the cocking handle in place and prevent the bolt from going forward to fire the weapon. With the safety catch disengaged, pulling the trigger let the bolt go forward to fire the gun. The Lewis fired from an open bolt so that the chamber could cool between bursts; there was a perceptible change of balance as the bolt went forward, picked up the cartridge and rotated into battery, firing the round as it locked. This was less accurate than a closed-bolt system, in which the bolt is already forward with the bullet in the chamber when the trigger is pulled, and no movement disturbs the aim until the round has left the barrel and the bolt moves backwards to collect and chamber the next round. However, pinpoint accuracy was deemed less important than overheating in an LMG, and most later automatic weapons used the same system.

The .303 round was quite a powerful cartridge, but recoil was actually less than that of the Lee-Enfield rifle, partly because the mechanism tapped off some of the propellant gas, but mostly simply because it was absorbed by the much heavier weapon. Empty cartridge cases were ejected from the right side of the gun; guns on some aircraft and vehicle mounts were fitted with wire-stiffened canvas case-catcher bags to prevent spent cases getting into moving machinery.

Firing repeatedly from the same position at night was unwise, as it could attract return fire from German snipers, machine guns or even artillery. Harry Patch, the last living soldier to have fought in the trenches of World War I and the oldest man in Europe when he died in July 2009 aged 111, served as a Lewis gunner with 7th Battalion, The Duke of Cornwall's Light Infantry in 1917. He describes his Lewis team firing at half-heard German patrols out in no-man's-land while on night sentry duty:

Bob, as the no. 1, would fire half a magazine at them, then, straightaway, we would move from our position down the trench. It was important not to fire a magazine from the same position because the Germans could see the flash from the Lewis gun and take a bearing on the position. Firing again from that spot was asking for half a dozen whizz-bangs [German high-velocity artillery shells]. So we'd always move, perhaps twenty, perhaps thirty, yards either way in the trenches and have another go, and then perhaps, later on, you'd go back to the same part of the line again. (Patch & van Emden 2007: 79)

Firing from the hip

The Lewis could be fired from the hip, but the gun was notably muzzle-heavy, and the metal cooling shroud heated up rapidly, making it difficult to use as a forward handhold unless the gunner wrapped a sandbag around his hand as a heat absorber. The wide webbing sling issued with the gun did help to support the weight, and a stirrup-like grip that clamped around the cooling shroud was introduced after World War I. Despite these problems, the Lewis could be (and was) fired from the hip. Private Jack Cousins of 7th Battalion, The Bedfordshire Regiment describes it:

US Marines firing an M1917 Lewis gun from the hip, using an improvised sling to help support the weight of the weapon. Note that the gunner is holding the gun canted to one side, so that the drum doesn't snag on his uniform as it rotates. The second man holds the six-drum US magazine chest. (Tom Laemlein/Armor Plate Press)

We got into the front-line German trench and my instructions were to follow the communication trench back to the German lines. Well, I had my Lewis gun, my head down below the trench, my gun crew following behind with spare ammunition. Suddenly, I could hear voices in front: I knew that they were German. I stopped at the bend, and suddenly I saw, coming around the bend, Germans in single file. When they spotted me, they started to unsling their rifles, but I didn't give them a chance, and I drove my finger on the Lewis gun trigger, and with a burst from the gun, three or four of them dropped dead. The others threw down their rifles and came with their hands up. (Quoted in Levine 2008: 135–36)

Another problem was that the pan magazine rotated as the gun fired, and the gunner had to hold the gun away from his body and canted to the right to prevent friction against his uniform or equipment causing a stoppage. It was to avoid this, as much as because of the weight of the gun, that Brigadier-General James Jack, officer commanding 28th Infantry Brigade, advocated using two men to fire each Lewis gun when going forward in the assault in July 1917:

Since I think it imperative to prevent Germans who escape the artillery from coming into action at point-blank range, we are heavily manning our leading line with Lewis guns. Each gun is carried by two men, the first with arm looped round the muzzle to steady it, the second holding the butt to fire. We believe that an occasional spray of bullets, though not accurate, will keep the enemy under cover. (Jack 2000: 226)

Firing from the hip was inaccurate, and some gunners used a comrade's shoulder as a rest for the barrel. While this didn't actually allow firing on the move, it did allow the gun to be brought into action very quickly, with more accuracy than firing from the hip. Edward Lynch, serving with 45th (New South Wales) Battalion of the Australian Imperial Force, describes it being used in this way: '... eight or nine Fritz leave the far side of the wood and make a dash to get away from us. A Lewis gunner drops his gun across the shoulder of a mate, rips and rattles the Lewis into action and the little group of running men are writhing in the dust' (Lynch 2008: 269).

A Canadian Lewis gunner uses his No. 2's shoulder as a rest to fire at enemy aircraft in July 1917, although the unloaded magazines at his feet and the relaxed stance of the onlooker suggests this is a posed photograph. If the gunner remained standing, the same method could be used to fire at ground targets on the move. (© IWM CO 1551)

Accuracy

Some of the strongest opposition to the Lewis actually came from the most fervent advocates of the machine gun. In their view, one of the most important attributes of a 'proper' machine gun like the Vickers was that it could be fired on precise and pre-set lines from its solid tripod mount, thus creating a 'nerveless weapon' that eliminated human error caused by fear and tiredness, which could reduce accuracy. These critics regarded the Lewis as a mere 'automatic rifle', though it was considerably more capable than other automatic rifles such as the French CSRG.

While the Lewis's open-bolt design meant that it was never going to succeed as a sniping weapon, it was never intended to be one, and there were few complaints from those actually using the weapon in its intended role. Indeed, Harry Patch – a good shot, but not one of the vaunted pre-war Regulars – describes using a Lewis gun to cut the bull's-eye from a target at 500yd with a single magazine for a bet, which suggests that the skill of the gunner, rather than the inherent accuracy of the weapon, was the main limiting factor (Patch & van Emden 2007: 132–33).

Reliability and stoppages

The Lewis gun was a complex weapon, and could suffer from a variety of stoppages, particularly in the muddy conditions of the Western Front. This complexity is illustrated by the 1940 manual *The Lewis Gun Mechanism Made Easy*, which lists 15 stoppages the Lewis could suffer, grouped by the position of the cocking handle when the gun stops. By contrast, the equivalent manual for the Bren gun, which replaced the Lewis, lists only eight possible stoppages. Harry Patch recalls:

> Because we were Lewis gunners and relieved of the jobs that the infantry were expected to do, almost our entire occupation was making sure that the machine gun functioned properly. The main problem with the machine gun was an unexpected jam at a vital moment. As a bullet travelled up the barrel, gas was sucked back on to the piston, forcing it back ready for the next round. However, should the gun get too hot, the piston wouldn't come back and compress the recoil spring and it was that recoil spring that was used to fire the next round. As it was my job to sort out any problems, I might have to replace the barrel, no easy job when the metal was hot enough to blister your fingers.
>
> If it was raining, we wore a groundsheet which we could use as a cape, but it was more important to keep the gun dry and we'd cover that first before we covered ourselves. The Lewis gun was our job – lose the gun and we lost the point of our being there – so our main concern was to make sure the gun was clean, oiled and ready for immediate use: loaded, magazine on ...
>
> The officers were very particular that the gun and the spare parts were kept scrupulously clean, otherwise you were put on a charge. If any of the brass cartridges were damaged, then they wouldn't be ejected from the gun, jamming it; likewise a little bit of mud could render the gun unusable, and there was plenty of that around, so they

were ensuring that we were ready if the Germans mounted an attack. (Patch & van Emden 2007: 74–76)

Keeping the gun in working order took considerably more attention than with a modern machine gun; each crew was issued with a spring balance to check the tension on their gun's mainspring, for example, and No. 2s labouring under the weight of the heavy (15lb) spare-parts bag often believed that it held enough spares to build a complete new gun from scratch. Training Lewis gun crews to deal with the various stoppages was a key part of the two-week training course, and crews practised it until it became second nature. Harry Patch described joining his Lewis gun team for the first time:

Cleaning and caring for the gun and its accessories took up a great deal of any Lewis team's time. Here the gunner checks the mechanism of his weapon while one of the crew loads rounds into a magazine in the front-line trenches near Cambrai, February 1918. (Cody Images)

As a no. 2 on the team, I would be responsible for carrying the spare parts for the machine gun, enough to build another one if needs be, and so I was not expected to cart around a rifle, too.

A sergeant introduced me to my new friends. At the time, the battalion was out of the line and we were sent to work on the ranges, training, to see how quickly we could do the job. I'd been thoroughly rehearsed on how to take a Lewis gun apart, and, if it jammed, what I could do. What I didn't know, Bob Haynes, the no. 1 on the gun, soon taught me. He insisted absolutely, 'You've got to be quick and accurate, our lives and your life depend upon it', and he kept on practising me, when out on rest, changing the magazine and stripping down the gun. I had to know what to do automatically when anything went wrong. (Patch & van Emden 2007: 71)

Others were less optimistic about the possibility of carrying out some of the more complex stoppage drills under battle conditions. Corporal Harry Fellows served on the Somme with 12th Battalion, The Northumberland Fusiliers:

It was a very delicate gun. You only had to have the slightest bit of dirt in it, and you had a stoppage. In our training, we were shown a drill to run through 'Number One Stoppage, Number Two Stoppage, Number Three Stoppage' and so on. I went on a course with about forty other NCOs, and the instructors were members of the Honourable Artillery Company. They were going through this drill, when suddenly an NCO jumped up, and he said 'I want to ask my

friends a question. When the Germans are coming at you, and your gun has seized up, have you ever gone through this drill?' Not one NCO said they had. The gun had a little wooden handle, called a cocking handle, and when the gun stopped, you put this handle in, and you pulled it back to reload the gun. You fired again, and if it didn't fire this time, you dumped the bloody gun. That was all there was to it. When the Germans were attacking you, and you were looking into their eyeballs, how could you start doing a drill? It was the last thing you were thinking of. (Quoted in Levine 2008: 41)

A British Lewis gun crew with a French officer on the Western Front. The leather jerkins and trench waders were needed to cope with the wet and muddy conditions in the trenches, which also meant the section's Lewis gun needed constant attention. Note the metal Lewis gun magazine boxes behind the men. (Cody Images)

No matter how carefully maintained, any Lewis gun used for sustained fire would seize up as it overheated. As the 1918 manual *Tactical Employment of Lewis Guns* explained, 'The Lewis gun is air-cooled, and will get over-heated when about 700–800 rounds have been fired rapidly. After about 1,000 rounds it will probably stop, and will take half-an-hour to cool.' It also notes: 'Individual Lewis guns vary greatly in this. There are records of certain Lewis guns firing 2,000 rounds with little cessation; a new gun will usually heat much more quickly owing to greater friction. Experiments carried out with selected guns, well supplied with oil, show that the stopping point usually occurs after 800–1,000 rounds' (War Office 1918: 4).

Poison gas affected the mechanisms of all machine guns, and crews were advised to fire occasional short bursts in the general direction of the enemy during gas attacks, to prevent their guns seizing up and for their 'moral effect', and to clean and re-oil the guns carefully afterwards. Cartridges were more seriously affected, as the gas caused them to corrode and cause stoppages. The steel magazine chests could be made more-or-less gas-tight using flannelette supplied for gun cleaning, but the canvas carriers gave less protection, and the open-bottomed magazines themselves offered none. Any magazine exposed to gas had to be emptied and the cartridges laboriously cleaned by hand before being used again.

BRITISH AND COMMONWEALTH INFANTRY SERVICE

The Lewis gun and the infantry battalion

The basic unit of British tactical organization during World War I was the battalion, containing about 1,000 men and commanded by a lieutenant colonel. Each battalion consisted of four companies, generally led by captains, and each company consisted of four platoons of about 50 men, led by lieutenants. Each infantry battalion initially had a two-gun Vickers machine-gun platoon as part of Battalion HQ, though at the start of the war some battalions were still equipped with the older (and heavier) Maxim guns, rather than the newer Vickers. This was increased to four Vickers guns per battalion in February 1915, after the machine guns had proved their value in combat.

From October 1915, however, these Vickers guns were stripped out of the infantry battalions and centralized as brigade machine-gun companies of the newly created Machine Gun Corps. Each infantry battalion received four Lewis guns in return, an exchange many were unhappy with, since the Lewis was initially regarded merely as an inferior version of the Vickers, rather than a new kind of weapon. Lewis gun allocations increased as the weapons became available, though the initial priority was to provide guns for new units as the Army expanded, rather than to increase the number held by existing units.

The 1914 platoon had consisted of four identical sections, each of a dozen riflemen under a corporal. By the time of the battle of the Somme in mid-1916, each infantry battalion should have had 16 Lewis guns, or one per platoon, though some had yet to receive their full allocation. Each section of the platoon had now adopted a specialized role, so that the platoon contained a section of riflemen, a section of 'Bombers' equipped with hand grenades, a rifle-grenade section and a Lewis gun section.

By late 1918, supply of Lewis guns had increased until each infantry battalion was provided with 36 guns, two per platoon plus four additional guns held by Battalion HQ for anti-aircraft use. Each platoon now consisted of two Lewis gun sections and two rifle sections, with the latter also carrying hand and rifle grenades. This organization continued until the Lewis was replaced by the Bren gun in the late 1930s and the platoon was reorganized into three sections, each containing a Bren and riflemen.

Becoming a Lewis gunner

Until the establishment of the Machine Gun Corps in October 1915, each British and Dominion infantry battalion provided the crews for its own Vickers and Lewis guns. After that, the Vickers guns and their crews were centralized into independent machine-gun companies at brigade level, but Lewis gunners continued to be drawn from their parent infantry battalions. The General Staff pamphlet SS122 *Some Notes on Lewis Guns and Machine Guns*, published in September 1916, offers advice on selecting men for the job: 'Company officers, in selecting men, should imagine that they have a new motor car and wish to choose one of their men to be trained as chauffeur. A Lewis gun is a

An Australian Lewis gun crew in the snow, on the Western Front in early 1917. It is unusual (though far from unique) to see a Lewis on a tripod this late; most were mounted on bipods, to take advantage of their mobility. (Australian War Memorial P00826.007)

A USMC Lewis gun team. Note the wooden six-drum ammunition boxes carried by the rest of the team; unlike the British, who favoured webbing carriers and used metal boxes largely for transport, the US used wooden boxes for both roles. (Tom Laemlein/Armor Plate Press)

more delicate piece of mechanism than a motor car and needs more constant attention.'

Trainee Lewis gunners were usually selected from those who qualified as marksmen, scoring at least 130 points of a possible 200 during their rifle qualification. Such men were relatively common in the British Army of 1914, made up of Regulars trained under pre-war conditions; the Army had not forgotten the lessons of the Second Anglo-Boer War a decade earlier, and well over half the men in a typical infantry regiment would have been marksmen. Such a standard could not be maintained during the massive expansion of the Army in the first years of the war, with shortages of instructors, rifle ranges and even rifles for recruits to train with. Indeed, one of the reasons the Lewis became important was exactly because of the decreasing accuracy and effectiveness of infantry rifle fire as the last of the pre-war Regulars disappeared. By the time Harry Patch went through his basic training in the winter of 1916–17, men achieving marksman standard were scarce enough that almost all were utilized in specialist roles, rather than as regular riflemen.

> It was something to be given the [marksman's crossed-rifles] badge to wear on your forearm, but if the truth be told it was the 6d a day extra pay that I was after. Being a marksman meant one of two things: I could be a sniper or I could be sent to a Lewis gun team. I could never have been a sniper – it was far too cold and clinical – so I was sent for training on the machine gun. Here they gave us a badge to go on our sleeve, wreath of laurels with LG for Lewis gun in the middle. As I was to discover, the badge was known to the machine gun crews as the 'suicide badge', because if you were taken prisoner by the enemy then more than likely you would be shot.[2] (Patch & van Emden 2007: 66)

2   Lewis gunners were initially issued the same 'MG' badges as Vickers gunners, for which a one-off deduction of 1s 9d was made from their pay, but by 1917 a separate and distinct badge for Lewis gunners was being issued. The 'LG' badge was still issued in World War II, by which time the Lewis itself had been replaced by the Bren.

Aside from the 6d a day extra pay[3] (a significant incentive, when an infantry private's pay started at only a shilling a day), Lewis gunners were also exempt from the endless and exhausting fatigues other infantrymen had to perform, such as bringing up rations or providing men for carrying parties. In fact, this was less a privilege than because the Lewis team already had significant extra duties to perform in moving, cleaning and maintaining their gun, without any others being added on. It was also often forgotten in the realities of combat, as Harry Patch explains, describing the scene in a recently captured trench:

> While the bombers cleared the dugouts, we got busy reversing the trench, using our entrenching tools to move the firestep from one side of the trench to the other. As machine gunners, we were usually excused such duties, but not now. We worked as hard as everyone else, moving the sandbags from one side of the German parapet to the other, piling them up with an aperture for the Lewis gun in between, where we could sweep in case there was a counter-attack, because we were certainly expecting one. (Patch & van Emden 2007: 98)

A Lewis gun post on the Lys Canal in April 1918, about to meet the great German offensive. The metal ammunition box held eight magazines. Each compartment could hold one of the four-drum bucket carriers, or two of the two-drum webbing pouches, but it was common to see them used to hold loose magazines, as here. Note that although cartridges are visible through the bottom of the upside-down magazines, the drum actually on the gun has not been pushed down into place and the gun would not be ready to fire until this was done. (Cody Images)

The Lewis gun section

On paper, the Lewis gun section consisted of eight men plus an NCO, usually a corporal. In reality, casualties, manpower shortages and men being detached for other duties meant that they were usually somewhat under strength. Harry Patch recalls the Lewis section he joined as being five men strong including himself, while Corporal Harry Fellows, serving on the Somme with 12th Battalion, The Northumberland Fusiliers, was even worse off: 'I was the corporal in charge of the two Lewis guns in the company, and I had four men on each gun, when I ought to have had six. I went to the company sergeant major, to ask him

3   Before decimalization in 1971, there were 12 old pennies (written 12d) to the shilling, and 20 shillings to the pound (£).

if I could have four more men. He said that I could have two' (quoted in Levine 2008: 38).

In theory, all members of the Lewis section were supposed to be trained to take over the gun and keep it firing if the gun crew became casualties, but this was not always the case. Harry Patch joined his crew straight from training as the No. 2, which suggests that the other members of the crew had even less experience, and the two extra men Harry Fellows received appear to have been normal infantrymen without special training.

The No. 1 carried and fired the Lewis gun itself, and often combined this with being the section NCO. The No. 2, or assistant gunner, carried the spare-parts bag, changed the ammunition drum and helped the gunner deal with any stoppages. Both the No. 1 and No. 2 were armed with revolvers. These were usually .455 Webleys, but sometimes Colt New Service revolvers in the same calibre, 60,000 of which were purchased from the United States to make up for shortages of British-manufactured weapons.

Nos 3, 4 and 5 were ammunition carriers, each carrying between four and 12 drums for the Lewis gun, depending on the mission and the ground to be crossed. In addition to the Lewis gun ammunition, these men carried Lee-Enfield rifles and ammunition for them. In ideal circumstances, the section would also have two or three riflemen, armed with Lee-Enfield rifles. These men might carry a small number of spare ammunition drums, but their main role was to act as scouts and local security for the team, and they were intended to be more lightly loaded to preserve their mobility. The guns and ammunition were a heavy load for Lewis crews to carry, as Harry Patch notes: 'It was no mean feat carrying all your equipment into action in dry weather, but over boggy, shell-pocked ground it would be hellish' (Patch & van Emden 2007: 88). Harry Patch describes how his Lewis gun section worked together:

A Lewis gunner of the Royal Garrison Artillery with his weapon on a cartwheel mount for anti-aircraft defence, France, March 1918. Note that despite the mount, the gun is not fitted with anti-aircraft sights. (© IWM Q 10749)

I used to lie down on the left-hand side of the gun, and when Bob had fired the magazine I would take it off with my right hand and hand it back to number three. He'd then hand it back to be reloaded. The three people behind you would be reloading with fifty rounds again. Number five would pass up a new full magazine to me and I would put it on and wait for Bob to use it. The magazine was designed so that it would only go on in one way. There was a pin on the gun we put the magazine on, it went in on a seat, ready for the round to go in. As far as I remember there was a spring of some sort, and you had to press something to pull it off.

The gun could fire fifty rounds a minute. Bob was expert at it, he was so light-fingered he would fire a round and finish, or he would fire two as was needed. I managed to get down to three and never got down to one. Bob could fire from the hip, he would pull the gun from his shoulder, one hand on the trigger, the other on the barrel. He pulled the trigger and it was away. If you looked under the magazine you could see the cartridges. If any of those brass cases were dented at all, the piston, when it came around, wouldn't throw it out and the gun would stop. If you had a dirty cartridge or magazine the round you used wouldn't come out and the gun would stop. You'd have to get it out and pull the lever back by hand to get it going again ...

The Lewis gun was air cooled. After you had fired two magazines you could not hold that gun, it got too hot to handle really. That's why Bob would never fire a whole magazine if he could help it, because of getting the gun too hot. It took a couple of minutes to cool down. If the gun stopped it was my job to get out whatever part it had stopped for. Bob and I between us could strip down that gun in a matter of ten to twelve seconds. (Quoted in Arthur 2002: 227–29)

A US Marine training with a Lewis gun, giving a good view of the 'Light Folding Field Mount', soon superseded by the lighter bipod. The pose with the Lewis gun and mount is very similar to that used for the 'Go over the top with U.S. Marines' recruiting poster. (Tom Laemlein/Armor Plate Press)

Like any small unit, Harry's Lewis gun section became a tightly knit group: 'There were five in a machine gun team ... these boys were with you night and day, you shared everything with them. We each knew where the others came from, what their lives had been and where they were ... It's a difficult thing to describe, the comradeship between us' (quoted in Arthur 2005: 122–23).

Ammunition supply

Each Lewis gun team was issued a total of 44 drum magazines, though they might not carry all of these at all times, depending on the mission. Magazines could be tucked into haversacks or sandbags, but it was awkward to carry any significant number like this. A bucket-like canvas carrier with a fold-over top holding a stack of four magazines was issued in 1915, but was awkward to get magazines in and out of. In 1917, each of the ammunition carriers was issued a set of four circular webbing magazine pouches, linked by straps that went over the wearer's normal webbing like a waistcoat, so that two of the pouches sat against the wearer's back, below the pack, and two on the front. Each pouch could hold two pan magazines, though it was common to place only one magazine into each if the wearer had to cover difficult terrain. Though heavy, the load was at least relatively well balanced.

British Lewis gun teams bring up their ammunition handcarts near Fricourt in September 1916. The crews have improvised hauling ropes to make the cart easier to pull, and the cart itself is almost buried beneath the crews' webbing and packs.
(© IWM Q 4112)

Unfortunately, neither of these carriers provided much protection against mud, rain or damage in transit, so a steel magazine chest was also issued. This was a weatherproof metal box with leather handles and a wooden central divider. Each of the two compartments could hold either

The .303 cartridge

Although Lewis guns were produced in numerous calibres, the vast majority were chambered for the British .303 round (7.7×56mm Rimmed), even when produced for nations like France, Italy and Japan. The .303 Mk I was introduced in 1888 as a black-powder cartridge with a round-nosed bullet. With the invention of smokeless powders in the late 1880s, the filling was changed to cordite (so called as it was made from chopped-up 'cords' of nitrocellulose and nitroglycerine), creating the .303 Mk II. Mks III to V changed the bullet shape and jacketing for improved expansion when striking a target, but were withdrawn after the Hague Convention of 1899 restricted the use of hollow-point and expanding bullets.

The Mk VI was the last round-nosed bullet, replaced in 1910 by the Mk VII. This exchanged the original round-nosed 215-grain bullet for a lighter and ballistically superior 174-grain pointed bullet, with consequent increase in muzzle velocity.[1]

According to the *Field Service Pocket Book* issued to British officers in World War I, the Mk VII round would penetrate 58in of softwood, 18in of well packed sandbags, 14in of lime mortared brick or ¾in of mild-steel plate. The pointed shape of the new bullet also inevitably meant that the centre of gravity was well towards the rear, exacerbated by filling the forward third of the bullet with a plug made of aluminium, wood pulp or sterilized compressed paper instead of lead. This had significant effects on the wounding characteristics of the round. Although the bullet remained stable in flight due to gyroscopic forces imparted by the rifling as it travelled down the barrel, it tended to tumble as it hit flesh, inflicting significantly more tissue damage than a simple 'through-and-through' wound. Since this was a physical characteristic of the pointed high-velocity round, and the bullet was fully jacketed, this was quite within the rules set out within the Hague Convention, and the cartridge remained in service until the adoption of the 7.62mm NATO round in the 1950s.

1   A grain is 1/7000th of a pound. A 174-grain bullet weighs approximately 2/5ths of an ounce, or 11.3g.

Contents of limbered GS Wagon for Lewis guns

Four Lewis guns, @ 27lb	108lb
Four sets spare parts, @ 15lb	60lb
176 magazines, filled, @ 4½lb	792lb
Four sets of spare parts, @ 15lb	60lb
22 metal ammunition boxes, @ 8¼lb	182lb
Nine 1,000-round boxes .303 SAA, @ 75lb	675lb
Total	1,949lb

This table is taken from the January 1918 British manual *Tactical Employment of Lewis Guns*, but it will be noted that the original table shows 'four sets of spare parts' twice, and that the total of the individual items does not equal the total given. The author conjectures that this is an error, and one of the sets of spare parts should be replaced with the line 'Four wooden gun chests, @ 33lb each', which would remove both anomalies and correspond to what really seems to have been issued.

one of the bucket-type carriers, or two of the webbing pouches. However, it was most commonly seen filled with loose magazines, in two stacks of four. Although intended mainly for transport, and not carried forward in the attack, these boxes often appeared in forward trenches as a way of keeping ready magazines dry and mud-free.

In addition to the 2,068 rounds actually loaded in magazines, each Lewis section was earmarked a further 2,250 rounds of .303 ammunition available with the battalion, plus a further 2,000 rounds with the divisional ammunition column. Loose .303 ammunition was packed in cotton bandoliers each holding ten five-round rifle chargers, with 20 bandoliers to each case of 1,000 rounds. A major task for Lewis gun ammunition carriers was stripping the rounds out of the chargers and loading them into the pan magazines.

In order to carry all this weight, each section was initially issued with a small handcart. While it was obviously not useful in the trenches, it was intended to allow easier movement along roads. In fact, most people shared General Jack's poor opinion of it:

> The Lewis gun cart resembles a coffin (suitable for containing the body of their designer) mounted on two strong bicycle wheels with solid rubber tyres. It is so low-set that the men hauling and pushing it must crouch. Each of our carts used to be towed by a pack mule, and it was then sufficient for a couple of soldiers to merely balance the vehicle. But this labour-saving practice has recently been disallowed; why, I cannot conceive. (Jack 2000: 183–84)

From the beginning of 1917, the handcart was replaced by a limbered horse-drawn General Service (GS) Wagon per four Lewis guns. With one wagon per four guns, each battalion would require nine such wagons – taking up quite a considerable amount of road space – just for its Lewis teams, so one can see the logistical problems faced by staff officers trying to move such units along crowded and often shell-damaged roads.

Recovering lost guns

As well as providing weapons for the expanding Army, Lewis gun production had to replace guns lost in combat. Battlefields were scoured for lost weapons after major attacks – Harry Patch describes his battalion recovering 250 rifles and two Lewis guns during one such assignment – which were then repaired for re-issue (Patch & van Emden 2007: 103). General Jack described the steps taken to avoid losing guns taken into no-man's-land in September 1917: 'Our patrols are always accompanied by one or two Lewis guns ... In order, however, not to lose the guns should they be dropped in the dark owing to casualties, we tie a long rope to each – the loose end fastened near our wire – so that they may be dragged back or otherwise found and recovered' (Jack 2000: 170).

THE LEWIS'S TACTICAL ROLES IN INFANTRY COMBAT

By the end of World War I, British machine-gun doctrine was probably the most advanced of any army, with the Vickers gun specialists of the Machine Gun Corps regularly able to use their weapons for indirect-fire barrages like artillery, against targets plotted on maps. However, this was the product of years of learning and development by a specialist organization.

By contrast, British Army machine-gun doctrine in 1914 was unsophisticated, and few infantry officers truly realized the potential of the machine guns they had available as direct-fire weapons, let alone the technical expertise to use them for indirect fire. Battalion Vickers guns were routinely sited as part of the infantry firing line, rather than using their long range to place them in safer positions further back. In fairness, it is hard to see how things could have been otherwise – until one understands what a weapon can actually do in a given situation, it is difficult to train officers in the best way to use it, and nobody had real experience of using machine guns in a modern war.

The same problems occurred with the Lewis, not helped by the initial assumption that since the Vickers and Lewis guns were both machine guns, they could do the same things and should be used in the same way. This was worsened by initially mounting Lewis guns on Vickers-type tripods, so that they lacked the mobility of a bipod-mounted gun, without the ability to put out the heavy sustained fire of the Vickers. Even once it was understood that the Lewis was not merely an inferior Vickers, but a different type of weapon altogether, there was no clear idea of how it should be used. Manuals of the period often describe the Lewis gun as 'a weapon of opportunity', another way of saying that units would have to work out for themselves how they should best be used.

By the winter of 1916–17, however, enough experience had been accumulated for clearer guidance to be issued. Each battalion received a specialist Lewis gun officer as part of Battalion HQ, a counterpart of the bombing officer responsible for grenades. Although Lewis gun teams remained under the tactical control of their platoon commanders, the Lewis gun officer was responsible for their specialist training, and advised the battalion commander about the best way to utilize the weapons. The

instructional pamphlet *The Tactical Employment of Lewis Guns*, produced by the Army in January 1918, outlined five main tactical roles for the Lewis gun with the infantry.

Supporting fire for advancing infantry

The British Army never really adopted the 'walking fire' doctrine adopted by the French and US armies, whereby infantry armed with large numbers of automatic weapons would fire from the hip as they crossed no-man's-land, suppressing the defenders by weight of fire. Indeed, the same qualities that made the Lewis a better machine gun than the lighter French Chauchat and American BAR made it less useful for this sort of work. Instead, the British preferred to rely more on carefully timed 'creeper' barrages, coordinated with the advancing troops so that the barrage lifted just as the attacking infantry – following close enough behind the barrage that they risked casualties from their own shells – were ready to assault the enemy trench. Even so, there was still a need for fire support that could advance with the troops, and respond instantly to threats such as enemy machine-gun teams emerging after the barrage had passed over them.

Doctrine said that Lewis gunners should be behind the first wave, rather than being part of it, so they did not become casualties immediately and remained able to respond to threats. They might fire from the hip, but this was acknowledged to be much less accurate than moving in bounds, and setting up the gun on its bipod to fire. However, the latter method made it very difficult to keep up with steadily advancing troops, and was only to be preferred when dealing with a significant threat such as a pillbox or machine-gun team. Sergeant Ernest Bryan, serving with 17th Battalion, The King's (Liverpool Regiment), describes using his gun this way during the battle of the Somme in 1916:

A Lewis gun team of The South Wales Borderers in Macedonia, September 1917. British and French troops had initially been deployed to Salonika to assist the Serbs, but this was made impractical by Bulgaria's entry into the war on the side of the Central Powers. By 1917, seven British divisions were serving on the Macedonian front, preventing the Central Powers from extending influence into Greece. These men, in sun helmets and with the Service Dress tunics removed to expose the collarless 'greyback' shirts beneath, found themselves fighting a very different war from their better-known colleagues on the Western Front. (© IWM HU 88189)

Mounts and accessories

At first, the Lewis gun was issued with the same heavy (48lb) tripod as the Vickers gun, which limited the Lewis's mobility and invited unfavourable comparison with the heavier gun. It was soon replaced with a 6lb 'Light Folding Field Mount' resembling a rigid bipod with a bracing bar, then a much lighter (3lb) folding bipod, which quickly became the norm. The cradle of the Vickers tripod could be reversed to mount the Lewis for anti-aircraft use, or a rather flimsy 'music stand' type anti-aircraft mount was issued. There was even a special monopod anti-aircraft mount with a spike, to allow the gun to be quickly fixed to a convenient post or tree stump.

A number of accessories were issued for the Lewis, including anti-aircraft sights, slings, a magazine-filling tool to speed up the task of loading dozens of magazines, a canvas breech cover to keep mud out of the mechanism when not in use and leather panniers to allow cavalry units to carry the gun on a pack saddle. There was even a shorter butt for guns issued to 'Bantam' battalions, made up of men below the standard minimum height of 5ft 3in, but otherwise fit and healthy. Aerial guns had their own accessories, including the Veeder Counter, which sat atop magazines to show rounds remaining, muzzle boosters to increase rate of fire and electric gun-heating units to prevent aircraft guns from freezing at high altitude.

An Australian Lewis gunner near Port Moresby, Papua New Guinea, in 1942. Although the gun is set up on the rather flimsy 'music stand' anti-aircraft tripod, no anti-aircraft sights are fitted, and no spare ammunition is visible, suggesting a posed photo. (Australian War Memorial\ P04960.002)

I was carrying a loaded Lewis gun, weighing just under thirty pounds. When we got towards their front line, up pops their machine gun, and chained to this gun was a German.[4] The first thing I did was sling my Lewis gun under my arm and press the trigger. The German gunner went down; whether he was hit or not I didn't know and I didn't care, he was down. I sprayed right along the top, to keep the Germans' heads down. That gave us a chance of getting in. (Quoted in Levine 2008: 139–40)

The machine-gun killer

The Lewis was often viewed as the answer to the tactical problem of enemy machine guns, which had superior firepower but were much less

4   Accounts of German machine-gunners being chained to their guns occur in several British and Dominion sources. This often came from seeing the leather hauling straps German MG 08 gunners attached to their webbing to help move their guns. However, Edward Lynch describes a case where a German machine-gunner actually did chain himself to his weapon and throw the key out of reach, for fear that his nerve would break and he would shame himself and his regiment by abandoning his weapon.

mobile. The Lewis gun had the advantage of mobility, and a much lower profile since it could be fired from a prone position, exposing much less of the gunner than the German MG 08. Lewis gun teams – or perhaps only the gunner and one or two others – would slip out of the British trenches, and move out into no-man's-land to take up position in a shell hole, and stalk the opposing machine gun as a submarine stalks a battleship – to use the metaphor employed by one Army pamphlet, SS122 *Some Notes on Lewis Guns and Machine Guns*, from September 1916 – delivering a sudden and devastating surprise attack before its opponent could bring its superior firepower to bear. This was often coordinated with other activities such as trench raids, so that the Lewis team, unseen in the darkness, would be able to sight in on any German gun firing on the raiders. On other occasions, distractions were deliberately created to draw German fire and give the Lewis gunners a target.

The Australian Edward Lynch describes several Lewis teams being sent into no-man's-land at night, to cover pioneers and infantry digging a new trench line ahead of an existing one. The work went well at first, until a careless noise from one of the diggers attracted fire from a German machine gun:

> … Fritz lets go another burst and we hear a very distinct *pinggg* as a bullet ricochets off a spade or something at the new trench.
>
> Another burst and a sharply cut-off yell of pain from our digging party.
>
> 'Blast him! He's got someone!' The Fritz hears the yell and opens up an extra long burst.
>
> The O.C. [Officer Commanding] grabs my arm hard. 'There! Not fifty yards away! I saw the men behind the flash of the gun. Get Corporal Taylor here with his gun as fast as you can.' (Lynch 2008: 100)

The narrator fetches Taylor (the crack shot of the unit) and his Lewis gun team from their post further along the line:

> We reach the captain, and drop down in the mud with him to listen and look for Fritz's gun.
>
> 'He heard that yell,' whispers the O.C. 'He'll fire in that direction all night. His shots aren't crossing here. Get your gun steady and sight it on his flashes.'
>
> They mount the gun and the O.C. aims it in the direction of the enemy gun. Then he makes way for Taylor who squats down in the mud behind the Lewis. Another burst during which Taylor is busy sighting at the fiery dancing glow out there in the dark.
>
> 'I'm right on to him, Sir.'
>
> 'Let him have it next time he fires.' And we sit waiting and watching through the darkness, too keyed up to breathe comfortably. Snowy Taylor is down behind his gun and his crew in position. If Taylor misses, we can expect dozens of enemy bullets fair amongst us here.
>
> 'Blast you, Fritz! Open up!' whispers a man, and as if in answer straight away comes *Crack! Crack! Crack!* We are looking at the

enemy gun! Behind its jumping glow we can make out three or four men. Isn't Taylor ever going to fire? Fritz will stop and the chance will be gone perhaps forever! Why doesn't he fire? *Bang! Rat-ata-tat-tat* and Taylor's little gun is quivering and jumping and we can actually hear its bullets fairly rattling on the Fritz gun out there in the blackness. Two separate yells – startled, frightened yells of pain – come across above the rattle of Taylor's firing. He pours a whole magazine of bullets in – burst after burst – and stops, and his men change magazines like lightning, but it's all over. Snowy has got that gun fair and square. (Lynch 2008: 101)

Consolidation of captured ground

German doctrine required an immediate counter-attack whenever a position was lost. While it was possible to use barrages from artillery or Vickers guns behind the line to interdict or break up such counter-attacks, British troops had to be ready to switch very quickly from attack to defence when they captured a German trench. Since German artillery was inevitably already pre-ranged on their own trench lines for exactly this circumstance, packing a captured trench with enough men to repel an assault by rifle fire was an invitation to receive appalling casualties. The obvious solution was to use a lesser density of riflemen, but supplement their firepower with machine guns.

Vickers guns were too heavy to haul forward with the attacking infantry, and took some time to set up as a new position had to be cut for it in what had previously been the back wall of the trench. By contrast, the Lewis gun could go forward with the infantry waves and be ready for use almost immediately, with no more preparation than a rifle.

Defending captured positions was one of the main reasons that Lewis teams were issued so many magazines, as they might have to hold the captured position until reinforced, perhaps not until nightfall. The Australian soldier Edward Lynch describes the scene in a newly captured trench:

Our Lewis gunners are setting up their guns in feverish haste lest the counter-attack develop before they are ready to stop it. Every few

The Lewis gun section (previous pages)

By the time of the third battle of Ypres in August 1917, the British Army had integrated the Lewis gun down to platoon level, in a specialized section containing the two-man gun crew, ammunition carriers and a pair of riflemen to act as scouts and local security. Lewis gun sections were normally deployed in the second wave of an attack, so that they could deal with German machine-gun teams emerging from deep dugouts to defend pillboxes and shell holes after the moving 'creeper' artillery barrage had passed over them. The Lewis gun section members seen here are less burdened by consolidation stores than the infantrymen advancing behind the Mk IV tank (a 'female' with two Lewis guns in each side sponson) but make up for it with the extra ammunition drums carried in the circular webbing carriers on their equipment.

yards a man is on duty watching the enemy positions to see what is to happen. All spare men are shovelling and digging at breakneck speed to repair the trench. Sandbags are being filled and carried to Lewis gun positions or used to top off the rim of the trench. (Lynch 2008: 79)

A Lewis gun team setting up behind the minimal cover of a railway embankment during the battle of Hazebrouck in April 1918. The No. 2 (to the left of the picture, holding a spare drum ready) has taken off the four circular Lewis gun drum-pouches he carries, and laid them in front so that he can get at the ammunition more quickly. (Cody Images)

Strengthening front-line defensive firepower

By the middle of the war, Vickers guns dug in behind the immediate front line provided most of the direct fire defending the British trenches, sited to cover carefully interlocked fields of fire. However, irregularities in the terrain – slopes, shell craters and so forth – inevitably created dead ground that could not be swept by fire from these guns. Equally inevitably, an enemy with the tactical skill of the German Army would attempt to make use of this dead ground, and rifle fire alone was unlikely to be enough to stem a determined assault.

The ideal solution was to pre-register the dead ground for friendly artillery, so that a colour-coded 'SOS' rocket fired from the trenches would call down a barrage to break up any assault. However, artillery might not always be available, or might already be firing on another SOS mission, and some areas of dead ground were too close to British positions to call down artillery without a high risk of friendly casualties. Lewis guns, therefore, were used to cover areas that the Vickers could not, and to bulk out the rifle fire of the defending infantry, which could be just as important for its morale effect as its physical one. Private Frank Dennis of 6th Battalion, The King's Own (Yorkshire Light Infantry) describes repelling a German assault, preceded by an artillery and gas bombardment, in 1917: 'By a miracle we have two Lewis guns that still function, and we put up concentrated rapid fire. Fritz wavers, re-forms and keeps coming nonetheless. Lights are improved by now; not so much wasted fire, and the Squareheads go down like ninepins. What are left are crumpling and endeavouring to retreat' (quoted in van Emden 2008: 281).

53

The Lewis as an anti-aircraft weapon

The increasing threat posed by aircraft led the British Army to issue a number of patterns of anti-aircraft sights for the Lewis. All featured a large ring to allow rapid acquisition of fast-moving targets. Firing directly at aircraft was useless, as by the time the bullets reached the point of aim, the aircraft would be several hundred feet ahead of that point, so the sights were designed to help the gunner 'lead' the target, that is, aim ahead of it so that it flew into the stream of bullets. These pictures (based upon those in a 1920 manual) show how these sights were used.

(**1**) The large front ring clamped onto the barrel jacket, and folded down when not in use. The much smaller back sight ring is shown within the clamp ring.

(**2**) ON TARGET! The outer ring was intended for aircraft at higher altitude (500–3,000ft); if the gunner ensured the target aircraft was flying towards the centre bead, with its nose touching the outer ring with the point of contact centred in the back sight, the bullets

should hit the aircraft.

(**3**) OFF TARGET. Although the aircraft's nose is touching the outer ring in the centre of the back sight, it is not flying toward the centre bead, and the bullets will pass below the aircraft.

(**4**) OFF TARGET. Although the aircraft is flying toward the centre bead, its nose is not touching the outer ring. The gunner has opened fire too early, and the bullets will pass in front of the aircraft.

(**5**) OFF TARGET. Although the nose of the aircraft is touching the outer ring, the point at which it touches is not centred in the back sight. The bullets will pass in front of the aircraft.

(**6**) ON TARGET! The inner ring was intended for low-flying targets (less than 500ft), but the other rules remained the same – the point where the target aircraft's nose touched the inner ring still had to be centred in the back sight, and it still had to be flying towards the central bead.

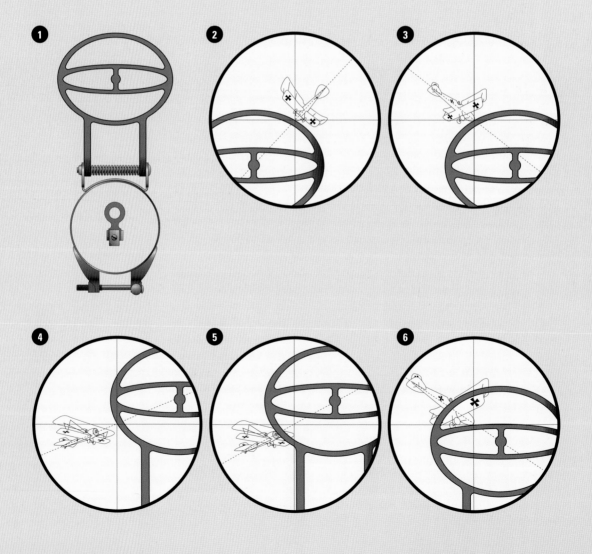

An anti-aircraft Lewis manned by Indian troops in Mesopotamia in 1918; the alacrity with which the troops in the background are taking cover suggests this may not be a drill. Note that the pit has been dug so that the gunner can move his weapon through 360 degrees. (© IWM Q 24781)

Air defence

While infantry had always tried to shoot down enemy reconnaissance aircraft, air defence became increasingly important with the appearance of dedicated ground-attack aircraft. Rifle-calibre bullets were reasonably effective against the relatively slow, flimsy aircraft of the period, and by the end of 1918, four of the 36 Lewis guns allocated to each infantry battalion were kept as part of Battalion HQ rather than issued to platoons, and were used for air defence. Such guns were supplied with special anti-aircraft sights, and fitted to a variety of mounts. A common improvised mount was created from a cartwheel and axle with the lower wheel buried and the Lewis gun attached to the upper one, allowing quick traverse.

Even without such sights and mounts, infantry were quite willing to engage low-flying aircraft, perhaps as much for the sense of hitting back as for any serious expectation of a hit. 2nd Lieutenant Harold Jones, serving with 2nd Battalion, The South Wales Borderers in 1918, describes an occasion when ground fire was successful despite the lack of a proper mount:

> Enemy aeroplanes were flying low and firing their machine guns at all and sundry. One woman was killed on her doorstep. The plane that did this flew over our farmyard and holding a Lewis gun on a man's shoulder and another at the trigger we gave it a magazine at point-blank range and to our joy brought it down in the adjoining field. The two occupants set it on fire before we could get to them and then kameraded in the approved style. They put on quite the 'Conquering Hero' air and demanded an officer's escort. We had a dickens of a job to stop the men putting paid to their account. (Quoted in van Emden 2008: 342)

A Chevrolet truck of the Long Range Desert Group in 1942. It has specialized equipment for desert travel, and the three-man crew have fitted it with a Lewis gun on the rear pintle and a salvaged or captured Italian Breda machine gun in front of the passenger seat. (© IWM E 12380)

OTHER ROLES FOR THE LEWIS

The Lewis gun as a tank gun

The Lewis saw its first use as a vehicle-mounted gun within weeks of the start of the war, when an armed touring car of the Royal Naval Air Service (RNAS) car patrol used one of the prototype Model 1913 guns to engage a German cavalry patrol in September 1914. The later Rolls-Royce armoured car was normally armed with a Vickers gun in the turret, but some would acquire Lewis guns in the interwar period, either in addition to or instead of their original armament.

The first British tank to see action, the Mk I of 1916, was armed with a Hotchkiss LMG in the nose plus either a 6-pdr (57mm) gun and a Hotchkiss LMG in each sponson ('male' tanks) or two Vickers guns in each sponson ('female' tanks). However, the strip feed of the Hotchkiss proved impractical in the close conditions of a tank interior, forcing the feed strips to be cut down to hold an inadequate 14 rounds each. Meanwhile, the belt feed and cooling tubes required by the Vickers guns meant that two of them were extremely crowded in a single sponson, and the armoured covers required to protect the water jackets from shrapnel unbalanced the mounts, making them clumsy to traverse.

The Mk II–IV tanks thus replaced both Hotchkiss and Vickers guns with ball-mounted Lewis guns, before the designers reverted to the Hotchkiss – now fed from the improved articulated belts – for the Mk V and Whippet. The reason usually given for replacement with the Hotchkiss was that the relatively large-diameter Lewis barrels were often struck by bullets, though the cooling shroud around the barrel of a Lewis gun was not essential to its operation and the gun should have continued to fire with the shroud holed by bullets.

Tank crews also complained that the cooling slots inside the Lewis shroud brought fumes, gas and dust from outside the tank directly into the gunner's face. This seems odd, given that early tanks were not gas tight and the atmosphere inside was so foul that crew occasionally passed out from asphyxiation, so one wouldn't imagine that dust blowing in from outside would have made it very much worse.

Tanks typically carried a spare Lewis gun aboard to replace weapons put out of action by damage or overheating, and quite prodigious amounts of ammunition – Mk IV 'females' each carried 30,082 rounds of .303 ammunition, or more than 6,000 rounds per gun. 'Males' carried only 6,272 rounds of .303, plus 332 6-pdr shells.

A lengthened version of the Mk V tank (known as the Mk V*) was created in 1918. Although the increased length was purely to allow it to cross the wider trenches of the Hindenburg Line, there were plans to use the additional 6ft of internal space to carry a Lewis team forward under armour, to dismount and fight on foot once the German trenches were reached. Unfortunately, the experiment proved that after their ride in the lurching, windowless and asphyxiating passenger compartment, the Lewis team were in no condition to fight effectively once they arrived. Crews of tanks put out of action by damage or mechanical breakdown were used as dismounted Lewis gun teams during the great German offensive of 1918.

The machine guns fitted to World War II tanks were generally coaxial guns mounted alongside the main armament. The Lewis's drum feed was ill suited to the tight spaces such guns had to fit into, and it was replaced by other designs.

The Lewis as an aerial gun

The Lewis was the first machine gun to be fired from an aircraft, although the US General Staff dismissed it as a publicity stunt, stating they envisaged military aircraft being used only for reconnaissance. Similar experiments in Belgium and Britain the following year were much more positively received by their respective governments, however.

Once war began, the Lewis was quickly pressed into service to replace the pistols and rifles first used as ad hoc aircraft armament, its light weight and ability to feed at all angles giving a distinct advantage over other machine guns even before specialist air variants were developed. Indeed, most of the Lewis guns purchased by the British in the first year of the war were used as aircraft armament, rather than as ground guns.

Lewis guns were used in three main ways aboard aircraft. The simplest was as fixed forward-firing guns controlled by the pilot. Since the guns could not fire through the spinning propeller blades, such guns were usually mounted above the top wing of biplane fighters and fired via a Bowden cable attached to the trigger, so that the bullets travelled just above the propeller arc. The mount generally allowed the gun butt to slide or pivot backwards and down for reloading, and some pilots used this to deliver a surprise attack from below. This may have made up for the difficulty of reloading

A British Fleet Air Arm gunner with a Mk III Lewis. Note the simple aerial sights, and the leather grip fitted to the 97-round drum to facilitate handling while wearing thick flying gloves. The canvas case-catcher bag attached to the weapon is to prevent ejected cases damaging the engine or control surfaces, but was not always fitted. The Fleet Air Arm came into being in 1924 and remained under RAF control until 1939, when it passed to the Royal Navy. (Cody Images)

Lewis guns being issued to airmen of No 22 Squadron, RAF. The RAF was created in April 1918 by merging the Royal Flying Corps (previously part of the Army) and the Royal Naval Air Service (previously part of the Royal Navy). Note that the standing airman has a Mk III gun on his shoulder, while those leaning against the hut are Mk IIs. The airman at the rear may be loading magazines, or checking them for functioning before issue. (Cody Images)

these guns; as changing the magazine required both hands, the pilot had to grip the stick with his knees to do so, not ideal in a combat situation.

One can imagine the relief of pilots with the invention of chain- or cam-driven synchronization gear that allowed guns to fire through the propeller disc by coordinating the firing cycle of a gun mounted on the engine cowling with the engine speed, so that the bullets passed between the spinning blades. However, the Lewis gun's open-bolt design meant that the lag between pulling the trigger and the gun firing was too long for the precision timing necessary. Several closed-bolt conversions were tested for use as synchronized guns, but generally the role passed to other weapons such as the air-cooled version of the Vickers gun.

The second way of using the Lewis was as a flexibly mounted defensive gun, mounted on a pivot or ring mount such as the British Scarff mount and fired by an observer. These guns had the advantage that they could defend the vulnerable rear of the aircraft, where enemy fighters were most likely to attack, and the Lewis's magazine feed meant that it could be swung around without fears of tangling ammunition belts. A special oil was developed for the aerial gun, as conventional lubricating oils tended to congeal in the cold conditions of high-altitude flying and cause stoppages.

Fighter tactics (previous pages)

Albert Ball in action, May 1916. The Lewis's self-contained design and relatively light weight made it a natural choice to arm fighter aircraft, such as this Nieuport. However the limited size of the ammunition drum (even the double-size 97-round drum seen here) meant that some method of reloading in flight was essential.

The Lewis gun was normally mounted over the wing, so that the line of fire was outside the propeller arc when it was fired forwards, but could be pulled back along a sliding track to be reloaded. However, some British pilots, including the ace Albert Ball, found that they could use this to fire the Lewis gun upwards, stalking unsuspecting German aircraft from below to deliver a lethal close-range belly shot.

Ball was the first of the British aces to have their achievements deliberately used as a propaganda tool, and became a celebrity. He had 44 victories to his credit when he was killed in May 1917, making him the leading British ace at that point, though his total was eventually surpassed by a number of others. He was posthumously awarded the Victoria Cross.

Early in the war, similar mounts were also fitted in the nose of aircraft such as the Vickers FB5 'Gunbus', which used a rear-mounted engine and propeller as a solution to the problem of firing forward through the propeller. Since simple aerodynamics means that such 'pusher' aircraft were generally slower and less manoeuvrable than conventional aircraft, they had only limited success and disappeared once synchronized guns became available.[5] The Lewis served in the flexible defensive role on British, American and Japanese aircraft into the late 1930s and early 1940s, being finally superseded by guns with a higher rate of fire.

The third and least common way of utilizing Lewis guns was in dedicated 'trench strafer' mounts, such as those installed in a small number of modified Sopwith Camels, featuring a number of fixed, downward-pointing guns specifically for attacking ground targets. However, limited ammunition capacity and the need to fly straight and level to use them – making the attacking aircraft an easy target for ground fire – made this a relatively short-lived idea.

Fixed forward-firing guns generally had simple ring sights similar to the anti-aircraft sights supplied for ground guns, while flexible-mounted defensive guns generally had more complex sights, such as the British Norman Wind Vane Sight, which compensated for the speed of the aircraft according to the speed of the slipstream across the sight. In many cases, however, gunners found it simpler to aim by eye, using tracer bullets loaded as every fifth round.

Using the Lewis as an aircraft gun had some unique challenges, as both gunner and target were often moving rapidly in three dimensions. The supply of training aircraft was limited, so air gunners could only receive part of their training aloft. Air-gunnery training could also be unexpectedly

The pilot of a British SE5a fighter slides his Lewis gun back along the curved track of a Foster mount. Although the gun was normally locked to fire forward, by releasing the lock on the mount it could be pulled back and used to fire up into the belly of an unsuspecting enemy. This photograph is taken on the ground, but since the pilot needs one hand to pull the gun back and the other to handle the 97-round drum, the difficulty of reloading in combat is all too obvious! (Tom Laemlein/Armor Plate Press)

A gun camera. Shaped to resemble a Lewis gun, it was used to train air gunners during simulated dogfights. Pulling the trigger activated the camera shutter, allowing the gunner to see what he would have hit when the film was developed back on the ground. This example is a British Mk IIIH of 1916; other countries had similar devices. (Author's photograph, © Royal Armouries PR.7128)

5   The Gunbus was originally armed with a single Vickers gun, but problems with tangling ammunition feeds led to replacement with a Lewis gun.

A British Light Car patrol in Jerusalem, April 1920. The car's bonnet has been completely removed to help with cooling. Without the Lewis gun, these small patrols could not have carried enough firepower to be effective; the difficulties of using the water-cooled Vickers in the desert are self-evident. (Cody Images)

hazardous for both the trainee and his pilot, as Leading Mechanic Bill Argent discovered when he was posted to the RNAS Air Gunnery School at Eastchurch on the Isle of Sheppey in January 1917: 'I was waiting for my first flight in a Maurice Farman when I saw the lad in front of me go up and, with his Lewis gun, shoot away one of the struts!' (quoted in Arthur 1996: 95–96).

As a result, all nations developed aids to make such training cheaper and more realistic. The simplest of these were gun cameras, built to resemble Lewis guns, but loaded only with film. They were used in mock dogfights, to determine whether or not the gunner would actually have hit the opposing aircraft with a real gun. More ambitious simulators tried to simulate the speed and rapidly changing angles of flight without the expense of aircraft. The Canadians constructed a device with the gunner

in a cage that slid down a cable between two tall pylons, for instance, while in another slightly less hair-raising device, the gunner fired at targets while sitting in a simulated cockpit that ran down a curved and inclined narrow-gauge railway track like a roller coaster.

The Lewis as a naval weapon

Both the Royal Navy and the US Navy adopted the Lewis gun enthusiastically, fitting them to everything from armed trawlers to battleships. Even British submarines carried a single Lewis gun to mount in the conning tower when surfaced. They were primarily intended for air defence – often on multiple mounts – but were also issued to deal with enemy boarding parties and small craft. During World War II, the light anti-aircraft role was increasingly taken over by the more effective 20mm Oerlikon cannon aboard naval vessels, but Lewis guns continued aboard merchant ships and small craft until the end of the war.

A Lewis gunner of the Arab Legion, photographed during a parade to commemorate the anniversary of the Arab Revolt. Originally set up in the 1920s to provide an armed force for the Emirate of Transjordan (later Jordan), the British-officered unit fought alongside the Allies during World War II, and against the Israelis in the 1948 war. (© IWM E 586)

After World War I

The Lewis gun remained the standard British LMG throughout the 1920s and early 1930s, seeing service with both Regular British troops and the 'Black and Tans' in Ireland and in skirmishes on India's North-West Frontier.

It had theoretically been replaced in the British Army by the Bren in the late 1930s, but many second-line units still retained their Lewis guns at the start of World War II, particularly in secondary theatres such as the Middle East, where they were often seen on Long Range Desert Group trucks into 1942. At home, the heavy losses of Bren guns with the BEF led to 60,000 elderly Lewis guns being broken out of storage, and another 46,000 purchased from the USA for issue to the Home Guard. Many of both the stored guns and those purchased from the United States were former aerial guns, and many were in poor condition, as Alexander Barr of the Norwich Home Guard recalls: 'We had an old Lewis machine gun. It wasn't the normal infantry Lewis gun – it was an ex-aircraft gun. There were no end of stoppages because it had all these springs inside and they were always going wrong. I only got to fire it once because of shortage of ammunition' (quoted in Levine 2007: 76).

THE LEWIS IN OTHER HANDS

Both during and well after World War I, the Lewis saw combat with other forces all over the world, for example being used by both sides in the Russo-Polish War (1919–21) and the Irish Civil War (1922–23). Although generally regarded as obsolete by the end of World War II, the Lewis gun would be employed by both Israeli forces and the Arab Legion in the 1948 Arab–Israeli War, while captured Japanese Type 92 guns would go on to see use by Communist forces during the Korean War (1950–53).

Russian Lewis guns

One of Lewis's assistants made several trips to Russia between 1912 and 1914, and the Tsarist government purchased a small number of guns (presumably the early closed-bolt 1913 models) before the outbreak of war. Although no documentation survives, photographs dating from mid-1916 show Russian aircraft equipped with British Mk II aerial guns, and the first surviving order for 200 guns also refers to ammunition for the guns already in service. In January 1917, the Russian purchasing commission ordered 10,000 BSA Lewis guns in .303 British calibre, plus another 1,200 chambered for the Russian 'three line' (7.62×54mmR) cartridges. It is not known how many of these weapons were supplied before deliveries were stopped by the Russian Revolution in November 1917, but Lewis guns were used by all factions in the Russian Civil War that followed.

The Lewis in German service

The German Army was impressed by the lightness and rate of fire of the Lewis, christening it the 'Belgian Rattlesnake', and made systematic use of

Soviet seamen receiving instruction on the Lewis gun from British Royal Marine instructors. The guns were used to arm Soviet merchant ships, which carried Soviet timber to Britain and took back lend-lease munitions. (© IWM HU 87229)

it in a way they did not do with other captured Allied machine guns such as the French CSRG. Any Lewis guns captured were converted to fire German Mauser ammunition at a special factory set up in Belgium before being issued alongside the Danish Madsen, many to special 'Musketen-Bataillone' armed largely with LMGs. Others were used as air guns, and were actually listed as the 'official' armament of some German aircraft types. Overall, it is estimated that the Germans captured more than 10,000 Lewis guns in World War I. The captured guns became important enough that the standard (and very comprehensive) machine-gunner's course run by the German Army covered three weapons – the MG 08, MG 08/15 and the Lewis. It is perhaps surprising that the Lewis gun was not reverse-engineered and put into production in Germany. Some captured guns were actually recaptured by the British, and converted back to .303 for re-use, bearing both British and German conversion markings as well as their original markings.

In World War II, the Wehrmacht again captured a significant number of British and Dutch Lewis guns in 1940, and put these into service with occupation garrisons and other second-line troops as the MG 137(e) and MG 100(h) respectively, without changing the original calibres.

German troops with captured Lewis guns during the battle of the Somme in 1916. The soldier near the right edge has a four-drum Lewis magazine carrier over his shoulder, while others carry the early cylindrical water cans for the MG 08. Several men also wear the drag harnesses used to move the heavy MG 08s.
(© IWM Q 55482)

The Lewis in US service

Lewis guns were used on the Jeffery armoured cars used by the US Army during the 1916 punitive expedition into Mexico. Although the United States finally adopted the Lewis gun in 1917, almost none saw service in the trenches. Unable to manufacture sufficient guns, the US Army purchased French Chauchat machine guns, while the limited number of Lewis guns produced were diverted to arm aircraft. While this was a logical decision, as the Chauchat was available in quantity but could not be sensibly used as an aircraft gun, the Chauchat did not endear itself to US troops, especially in the dire .30-06 version. Most irritated were the

US Marines, who had actually received Lewis guns before the United States entered the war, and found themselves having to hand them in on arrival in France and receive decidedly inferior CSRGs in return, in the name of standardization with Army units. The Chauchat was replaced by the M1918 BAR, which arrived too late to influence the outcome of the war, but was a good design and produced in sufficient quantity to make any further purchases of Lewis guns for the US Army unnecessary.

The US Marines did retrieve their Lewis guns after the war, and employed them in the 'Banana Wars' in Central America throughout the 1920s and 1930s – including use in the King armoured cars employed in those conflicts – and in the bitter fighting in the Philippines in the first months after US entry into World War II. Heavy losses of equipment and the need to standardize with the Army saw Marine Corps Lewis guns replaced by BARs, and none seems to have seen combat after 1942.

US Marines photographed with a Lewis gun during the occupation of the Dominican Republic (1916–24), one of the 'Banana Wars', a series of US interventions in various Caribbean countries. (Photo courtesy of US Marine Corps)

The 6.5mm Dutch M.20 version of the Lewis. This is a cyclist's or motorcyclist's version, identifiable by the sights and carrying handle, which both fold close to the barrel for transport. Note the wire shoulder rest, folded over the butt for carriage. The unusual 97-round Dutch magazine can be seen clearly, along with the leather magazine carrier. (Author's photograph, © Royal Armouries PR.1136)

The US Navy had retained the Lewis as an air-defence weapon on a variety of craft. These saw combat when the US gunboat *Panay* was attacked off Nanking by Japanese aircraft in 1937. Although accepted as a mistake at the time, the incident may have been an intentional test of US resolve in the run-up to war. A few Lewis guns continued to serve aboard Navy and Coastguard craft throughout the war, with the last only being removed in 1946.

Dutch Lewis guns

The Netherlands remained neutral during World War I, but since that war had started with the unprovoked invasion of neutral Belgium, it was a nervous sort of neutrality. The Dutch tried to purchase LMGs commercially during World War I to boost their meagre stocks, only to find that the belligerent powers were too busy producing for their own needs to sell any. After the war, the Dutch began manufacturing their own Lewis guns under licence for both ground and air use as the M.20. Although only around 10,000 guns were manufactured in total, the Dutch produced a large number of variants (such as special models for armoured cars, motorcycles, cyclists etc), many of which differed only slightly and were produced in extremely small numbers. Unusually, some cavalry, motorcycle and cyclist variants were fitted with folding buttstocks; the absence of a spring running through the butt made the Lewis one of the few machine guns where this was possible. Meanwhile, the armoured-car models and some air versions were built with dual spade grips and thumb triggers, like a Vickers gun. Dutch Lewis guns were initially produced in their standard 6.5mm rifle cartridge, but after 1925, guns were produced chambered for the German 7.92mm Mauser cartridge, which was used only for machine guns in Dutch service. All the Dutch ground and air guns used 97-round drums, though there were some experiments with smaller drums since the big drum made the gun unbalanced for ground use.

Bizarrely, the Air Service of the Dutch Navy serving in the Dutch East Indies was equipped separately from the Dutch home fleet, and during the late 1920s, it used Dutch-manufactured Lewis guns in .303 British, to give common calibre with the Vickers air-cooled guns used as their primary aircraft armament. Meanwhile, after the Netherlands fell to the Germans, the Dutch colonial defence force (known as the Koninklijk Nederlands Indisch Leger, or KNIL, and not part of the Dutch Army) purchased Savage-manufactured Lewis guns in the American .30-06 calibre, which saw service against the Japanese.

Japanese Lewis guns

The Japanese Army and Navy had completely independent procurement organizations throughout the 1930s – indeed, they effectively had independent foreign policies, with the Army favouring expansion into mainland China over the Pacific strategy advocated by the Navy. There was no separate air force, with (characteristically) both Army and Navy developing an air capability independently of the other. The Navy adopted the Lewis in .303 British (referred to as 7.7mm in Japanese service) as the Type 92 from 1932. It served as a flexible defensive gun on naval aircraft, including the dive and torpedo bombers that attacked Pearl Harbor, as an air-defence weapon on small craft and as a ground gun for the Special Naval Landing Forces.

All Japanese-made Lewis guns had the enlarged trigger guard fitted on post-1918 aerial guns and cocked only on the left, like the US model. Most were fitted with spade grips, even on ground models. The Japanese Army also had a Type 92 machine gun, but this was a completely different weapon and shared the designation only because the Japanese Army and Navy both named guns by year of adoption, with '92' equating to 1932. Given the questionable reliability of the Japanese Army's LMGs, one must feel that they could have done worse than following the Navy's lead and adopting the Lewis as a ground LMG, too.

A Japanese Type 92 machine gun on a tripod. All Type 92 guns featured the enlarged trigger guard for use with gloves, and were essentially copies of the British .303 Lewis with some small changes of detail. The Japanese 7.7mm round was a straight copy of the British .303, and Type 92s could use captured British ammunition. (Tom Laemlein/Armor Plate Press)

IMPACT
Two world wars and a tactical revolution

Twin Mk III Lewis guns set up to defend an aerodrome during an anti-invasion exercise in 1941; note the skeleton butts added behind the original aircraft gun rear spade grips. The gun seems to be fitted with a case-catcher bag, unusually for a ground gun. (© IWM H 14005)

The Lewis was probably the best of the World War I LMGs, and remains the most recognizable today. The only plausible rival was the American BAR, which did not appear until right at the end of the conflict and was driven by a very different design philosophy, making direct comparison difficult.

One key impact of the Lewis was simply that it allowed Britain to equip the large new Army necessitated by the war. Unlike the continental powers, which already had mass armies backed by hundreds of thousands of trained reservists in 1914, Britain had only a small (if highly trained) volunteer force, and the small Territorial Army. With fewer than a dozen Vickers guns a week being delivered at the start of the war, the fact that the Lewis was ready to enter production immediately was vital. During the war, around 145,000 Lewis guns were produced, compared with just under 74,000 Vickers guns, making it by far the most numerous machine gun in British service. It also meant that the British forces started receiving significant numbers of LMGs from mid-1915, almost a year before any other army, and without the rushed design-work that led to issues with the French CSRG.

TACTICAL IMPACT

Ground combat

Infantry tactics were revolutionized several times over during World War I
– first by entrenchments and barbed wire, then by the new LMGs, bombs
and rifle grenades, and then a third time by the tanks and infiltration
tactics developed at the end of the war. The Lewis did not cause these
revolutions by itself, but was a key component of the second and biggest
revolution, the change in the make-up of the rifle platoon. At the start of
the war, the infantry platoon was made up purely of riflemen, with no
other weapons except the revolver carried by the platoon's officer. Faced
with an enemy machine-gun nest, it would have had little choice other than
a near-suicidal attempt to out-shoot or assault the gun, or hunkering down
to wait for support.

By the end of the war, the same platoon had added hand grenades, rifle
grenades and a pair of Lewis guns, massively increasing its firepower and
tactical flexibility. Faced with the same machine-gun nest, it had several
options to allow some elements to suppress the nest while other elements

Motorcycles were used for
reconnaissance by all sides early
in World War II, before armoured
cars were available, and also
provided a way of moving
machine-gun teams quickly
around the battlefield. These
sidecar combinations belong to a
Home Guard unit on exercise near
Exeter, in August 1941; the men
are using their anti-gas goggles
as improvised motorcycle
goggles. (© IWM H 12609)

closed to grenade range. Indeed, the Lewis gun had become so important that Lieutenant-General Ivor Maxse, one of the most successful British divisional commanders and later its Inspector-General of Training, could exclaim in February 1918 that, 'A platoon without a Lewis gun is not a platoon at all!' (quoted in Griffith 1994: 79).

> A Lewis Gun in the hands of good gunners will work as much destruction as fifty average riflemen. The 'rat-tat-tat' of a Lewis Gun has a great 'moral' effect. Against a machine gun a man stands little chance, and human flesh will not face it ... the Lewis Gun offers a very small target, and at 400 yards ... it is practically invisible. Hence it is very hard to pick up and knock out. A Lewis Gun gives a maximum volume of fire from a minimum of front. (War Office 1918: 1–3)

This extract from a British manual of 1918 shows that the users of the Lewis gun were in no doubt about its effectiveness on the battlefield, especially where concentrated firepower was needed; a Lewis team could slide stealthily into no-man's-land in a way that a whole platoon of infantry could not. Once there, they could shelter from return fire behind small scraps of cover, and swing the gun around to bear against new targets far more easily than a line of riflemen could be redeployed.

Air combat

Almost uniquely, the Lewis was also key to developments in a second tactical area, that of air combat. It was not only the first machine gun to be fired from an aircraft – it was so successful in this role that it was adopted by almost all the combatant nations, whether or not they used it as a ground machine gun. The Lewis was used on more World War I aircraft types than any other weapon, and continued in service in limited roles for another three decades, before finally being replaced by more modern guns.

IMPACT ON THE ENEMY

In a speech to the British House of Commons on 20 December 1915, just before becoming Prime Minister, David Lloyd George estimated that machine guns caused 92 *per cent* of the casualties on the Western Front. Unfortunately, like many of Lloyd George's statistics, this figure was a rhetorical tool rather than an actual fact; Lloyd George had significantly increased the supply of machine guns during his time as Minister of Munitions – though, characteristically, not by as much as he often claimed – and thus had a vested interest in portraying them as effective weapons of war.

In fact, casualty returns suggest that although the enduring image of World War I is of infantry being mown down by machine guns, around 60 per cent of casualties were actually inflicted by artillery. Even making the (highly likely) assumption that most of the remaining 40 per cent were caused by machine guns rather than rifle fire, Mills bombs and so forth, the majority of these machine-gun casualties are likely to have been inflicted by the heavier Vickers, rather than the Lewis. However, there are several things to remember when considering this.

German troops using a captured aerial Lewis gun on an improvised anti-aircraft mount. The photograph is undated, but must date from the last two years of the war. The Germans made extensive use of captured Lewis guns, even including them in their standard machine-gunners' course. (Tom Laemlein/Armor Plate Press)

73

Looking down the barrel – recruits of the Singapore Volunteer Force training with a Lewis gun in November 1941. Few units in the Far East had received Bren guns before the Japanese entered the war in December 1941.
(© IWM FE 214)

First, although other weapons may have inflicted more casualties, this still leaves the Lewis accounting for a very significant number. Second, while artillery and Vickers guns can inflict casualties, neither can take enemy-held ground. The Lewis – whether carried by infantry or mounted in the sponson of a tank – could do so, and this was ultimately as important as the simple numbers of casualties inflicted. Third, and perhaps most importantly, it was the only Allied machine gun to have registered sufficiently with the German soldiers for them to give it a nickname, the 'Belgian Rattlesnake', which does imply that they saw it as a more significant threat than other weapons they faced.

THE LEWIS'S TECHNICAL LEGACY

For a revolutionary and widely produced weapon, the Lewis left a surprisingly slender technical legacy, since many of its design features proved to be dead ends.

The distinctive forced-air cooling sleeve was copied in only one weapon, the Russian Fedorev-Degtyaryov of 1921, an LMG version of Fedorov's *avtomat* (automatic rifle) of 1916. The machine gun was produced in several variants, using simple air cooling, water cooling and a forced-air-cooling sleeve that appears to have been copied directly from the Lewis. In general, however, quick-change barrels of the type used on the Lewis's successor the Bren, or the German MG 34, provided a better technical solution to the problem of barrel overheating.

Colonel Lewis's last projects

Royalties from his most famous design made Lewis a wealthy man, but he continued to work on firearms designs almost up to his death. As early as 1916, Lewis had given his opinion that the US Army needed three models of machine gun: a heavy model capable of sustained fire; a second, lighter model to go forward with the attacking infantry, Lewis modestly noting that 'I believe the Lewis gun as at present in service use more nearly fulfils this important role than any weapon in existence now'; and 'a very light and portable machine rifle' (quoted in Easterly 1998: 515–16).

He began work on the third type of weapon on his return to the United States in February 1917, and over the next 16 months, produced three prototypes of his automatic rifle. The first bore a strong resemblance to a lightened Lewis gun, but the second and third were steadily lighter and more rifle-like, with the third prototype weighing only 12½lb. He also produced a single prototype of a 'shock action' automatic rifle – the name indicates the modified recoil operation of the weapon, not its intended use – with select-fire capability and a 20-round box magazine. Nothing came of these weapons, as by now the war was over and the army had already adopted the Browning Automatic Rifle, which almost exactly matched Lewis's own statement of what he wanted to build.

Lewis also produced a number of designs for .45 ACP pistols, including some with large 15-round double-column magazines. Given that the Colt M1911 was already in full production and the US Army was perfectly satisfied with it, however, very little official interest was shown in these designs.

A prototype of Colonel Lewis's 'shock action' rifle, capable of full- or semi-automatic fire. It fed from 5-, 10- or 20-round box magazines, inserted just ahead of the pistol grip. (Author's photograph, © Royal Armouries PR.5293)

The Lewis's rotating bolt group was used in the World War II German FG 42 automatic rifle, apparently to keep the development period of the new weapon as short as possible by using proven design elements where possible. The FG 42 was produced in an attempt to provide paratroopers with a lightweight select-fire weapon, and while it was really too light to be controllable when firing full-calibre 7.92mm Mauser ammunition on full-automatic, captured examples inspired several post-war US designs. The most important of these were the T44 (essentially an FG 42 modified with the belt-feed mechanism from an MG 42), and its successors, the T52 and T54. These led in turn to the M60, adopted as the US LMG through the Vietnam period and afterwards, which used a bolt and firing pin/piston assembly very similar to those on the Lewis.

Experience with the Lewis had shown up the problems with the odd clock-type mainspring all too clearly, and the idea does not appear in later weapons. Similarly, the open-bottomed pan magazine design, driven by the mechanism of the gun rather than internal springs, was not used again. Simpler box magazines gave less trouble, and though the drum magazine of the Soviet DP machine gun or the anti-aircraft drum produced for the Bren gun might look quite similar to the Lewis pan, they were actually quite different internally, having a bottom plate and internal springs to push up the cartridges like a box magazine.

CONCLUSION

World War I triggered numerous innovations, in everything from trench periscopes to poison gas. Many were specific to the nature of trench fighting, however, and did not significantly affect the way World War II was fought. Of those that did have more general application, the most significant (tanks and aircraft) appeared only in embryo, and still had much development ahead of them. By contrast, the new LMGs (along with hand grenades) emerged during the war almost fully developed. To put this into perspective, if an aircraft or tank of World War I appeared on a modern battlefield, it would be instantly ridiculous. If we replaced a modern infantry squad's general-purpose machine gun with a Lewis gun, however, they would still be able to carry out their battlefield mission, though they would find the weapon heavy and complex. Not bad, for a hundred-year-old design.

A US Marine instructor training Filipino troops on the Lewis gun in March 1942 on Corregidor, the largest of the four fortified islands protecting the mouth of Manila Bay in the Philippines. Note the British-style M1917 helmet worn by one of the recruits; issues of the more familiar M1 helmet had begun, but it was not universal by this date. (Tom Laemlein/Armor Plate Press)

The Lewis was certainly not a perfect weapon. It had significant shortcomings, as would be expected from a groundbreaking type of weapon, and it took time for armies to understand how it should best be used. However, the fact that it served throughout the two world wars, in almost every possible climate from the mud of the Western Front, to the heat and sand of the Middle East, to the freezing Atlantic seas and the cold of high-altitude air combat does suggest the strength of the basic design. It was used in almost every conceivable role – as an infantry-support weapon, an anti-aircraft gun, and as armament for tanks, aircraft, ships and even submarines.

It is also extremely striking that it was not only used by countries as diverse as Britain, France, the United States and Japan, but also that the Germans thought it was worth going to considerable trouble to bring captured examples into use, and did so in both world wars. Overall, it is hard to deny that the Lewis was well in advance of its competitors, as well as being technically and tactically groundbreaking. On the whole, it was extraordinarily successful for the first major weapon in its class, and deserves to be the most recognized of its generation of LMGs.

Gunners of the Royal Artillery man an anti-aircraft Lewis at Fort Crosby, near Liverpool, in August 1940. Note the anti-aircraft sight on the Lewis gun, and the crew members holding the rather flimsy 'music stand' anti-aircraft mount. All are still wearing the World War I-era 1908 webbing. (© IWM H 2695)

BIBLIOGRAPHY

'An Instructor' (1941). *The Complete Lewis Gunner, with notes on the .300 (American) Lewis Gun*. London: Gale & Polden.

Anonymous (1940). *Manual on the .300-inch Lewis Machine Gun*. Bradford-on-Avon: Bravon Ledger Co.

Armstrong, David A. (1982). *Bullets and Bureaucrats: The Machine Gun and the United States Army, 1861–1916*. Westport, CT: Greenwood Press.

Arthur, Max (1996). *Lost Voices of the Royal Navy*. London: Hodder & Stoughton.

Arthur, Max (2002). *Forgotten Voices of the Great War*. London: Ebury.

Arthur, Max (2005). *Last Post: The Final Word from Our First World War Soldiers*. London: Phoenix.

Bruce, Robert (1997). *Machine Guns of World War I: Live Firing Classic Military Weapons in Colour Photographs*. Marlborough: Windrow & Greene.

Chappell, Mike (1988). *The British Soldier in the 20th Century 4: Light Machine Guns*. Hatherleigh: Wessex Military Publishing.

Cornish, Paul (2009). *Machine Guns and the Great War*. Barnsley: Pen & Sword.

Easterly, William M. (1998). *The Belgian Rattlesnake*. Coburg: Collector's Grade Publications.

Ellis, John (1975). *The Social History of the Machine Gun*. Baltimore, MD: Johns Hopkins University Press.

Griffith, Paddy (1994). *Battle Tactics of the Western Front: The British Army's Art of Attack 1916–18*. New Haven, CT: Yale University Press.

Holmes, Richard (2004). *Tommy: The British Soldier on the Western Front*. London: HarperCollins.

Hutchinson, Lieutenant-Colonel G. S. (2004). *Machine Guns: Their History and Tactical Employment*. Uckfield: Naval & Military Press (originally 1937).

Jack, James L., ed. John Terraine (2000). *General Jack's Diary: War on the Western Front 1914–1918*. London: Cassell.

Levine, Joshua (2007). *Forgotten Voices of the Blitz and the Battle for Britain*. London: Ebury.

Levine, Joshua (2008). *Forgotten Voices of the Somme*. London: Ebury.

Lynch, E. P. F., ed. Will Davies (2008). *Somme Mud: The Experiences of an Infantryman in France, 1916–1919*. London: Doubleday.

Patch, Harry with van Emden, Richard (2007). *The Last Fighting Tommy: The Life of Harry Patch, Last Veteran of the Trenches 1898–2009*. London: Bloomsbury.

Popenker, Maxim & Williams, Anthony G. (2008). *Machine Gun: The Development of the Machine Gun from the Nineteenth Century to the Present Day*. Marlborough: Crowood Press.

Pridham, Major C. H. B. (1940). *Lewis Gun Mechanism Made Easy*, 6th Edition. London: Gale & Polden.

Royal Air Force (1918). *Instructional Notes on the Lewis Gun*. London: HMSO.

van Emden, Richard (2008). *The Soldier's War: The Great War through Veterans' Eyes*. London: Bloomsbury.

War Office (1917). *Method of Instruction in the Lewis Gun*. London: HMSO.

War Office (1918). *The Tactical Employment of Lewis Guns*. London: HMSO.

Woodman, Harry (1995). *Lewis Guns: Windsock Mini Data File 3*. Berkhamsted: Albatross Publishing.

INDEX